Praise for
A VOICE BECOMING

"Beth Bruno clearly has a heart for girls, and in this unique resource for mothers and daughters she bridges the two generations. With wisdom, humility, and heartfelt confessions, Beth offers a road map on how to celebrate our adolescent daughters while helping them discover their voice and purpose. In an age of intentional parenting, where moms hunger for guidance on how to raise strong, confident, and godly girls, this book meets an important need. Taken to heart, it can strengthen both families and society for many years to come."

—Kari Kampakis, mother of four daughters and author
of *10 Ultimate Truths Girls Should Know* and *Liked:
Whose Approval Are You Living For?*

"In A VOICE BECOMING, Beth Bruno celebrates the audacity of becoming a strong woman, offering a unique, intentional guide to helping your daughter plunge into womanhood. It's tempting to give up and just try to survive this tumultuous season, but A VOICE BECOMING provides practical ideas that go beyond simply enduring the teen years to relentlessly cultivating the hearts of our daughters."

—Melanie Dale, author of *Women
Are Scary* and *It's Not Fair*

"Fellow mamas, Beth Bruno is the wise guide we want on our team. And A VOICE BECOMING is the resource we've been waiting for to help us raise brave faithful young women. Her wisdom, passion, and love are precious gifts that nourish us and bless our girlies."

—Margot Starbuck, author of *Small
Things with Great Love*

"In her practical book, Beth Bruno helps mothers imagine their daughters' transition from girlhood to young adulthood differently, inspiring courage in place of fear, intentionality where there might otherwise be resignation. Besides offering wonderful recommendations of books and movies and activities to share together, Beth most importantly invites mothers into conversation and intimate relationship with their daughters. I only wish I'd read A VOICE BECOMING when my own two daughters were younger."

—Jen Pollock Michel, award-winning author of *Teach Us to Want* and *Keeping Place*

"A VOICE BECOMING is a rich, beautiful, trail guide for the mother who wants to lead her daughter into womanhood with intentionality and purpose. Laced with Scripture, story, and practical insights, Beth Bruno's book is one that I'll return to again and again as the mother of a daughter."

—Ann Swindell, author of *Still Waiting* and founder of Writing with Grace

"An intensely intimate look into a mother's fight for her daughter's soul and purpose. The challenges of modern life and influences are no match for this intelligent and creative resource. Pulling from memoir, biblical examples, literature, and real-life relationships, A VOICE BECOMING is decisively the resource for creating a life-changing rite of passage for your coming-of-age daughter."

—Shayne Moore, author and founder of Redbud Writers Guild

"Beth's book is a must-read for mothers, grandmothers, aunts, as well as fathers and grandfathers and uncles! I wish we had this guide raising our two daughters, but we now have two grand-daughters and the role we play is far more active in promoting the strength, voice, and character of our girls. This guide is a gift for all those who believe in our children's and grandchildren's future."

—Dan B. Allender, PhD, professor of counseling psychology, the Seattle School of Theology and Psychology, and Rebecca Allender, founders of the Allender Center for Trauma and Abuse

"Beth Bruno has lovingly created a compass for all those who long to find their way through today's tangled maze to adult-hood. A true north, A VOICE BECOMING is full of the very things we hope for each member of our global sisterhood whether she be mother, daughter, or friend—the blessing of knowing who we are, caring boldly for others, and the holy courage to *become* who we were always meant to be."

—Belinda Wilson Bauman, founder of One Million Thumbprints and author of *Brave Soul*

"Every mother longs for a kind, compassionate, and relatable friend to journey with her through the peaks and valleys of par-enting. In A VOICE BECOMING, Beth Bruno is that friend. She not only casts a compelling vision for who God designed girls to become but also calls us mothers inward to investigate our own voice, calling, and stories. You will find both a trajectory for your daughter as she enters womanhood as well as an invitation to participate in God's great story of global sisterhood."

—Aubrey Sampson, MOPS International blogger, speaker, and author of *Overcomer* and *Game Changer*

A Voice Becoming

A Voice Becoming

A Yearlong Mother-Daughter Journey into Passionate, Purposed Living

BETH BRUNO

New York   Nashville

FaithWords
Hachette Book Group
1290 Avenue of the Americas, New York, NY 10104
faithwords.com
twitter.com/faithwords

Originally published in hardcover and ebook by FaithWords in January 2018
First Trade Paperback Edition: December 2018

FaithWords is a division of Hachette Book Group, Inc. The FaithWords name and logo are trademarks of Hachette Book Group, Inc.

The publisher is not responsible for websites (or their content) that are not owned by the publisher.

The Hachette Speakers Bureau provides a wide range of authors for speaking events. To find out more, go to www.hachettespeakersbureau.com or call (866) 376-6591.

Library of Congress Cataloging-in-Publication Data

Names: Bruno, Beth, author.
Title: A voice becoming : a yearlong mother-daughter journey into passionate, purposed living / Beth Bruno.
Description: New York : Faith Words, [2018] | Includes bibliographical references.
Identifiers: LCCN 2017032373| ISBN 9781478974659 (hardcover) | ISBN 9781478974680 (ebook) | ISBN 9781478923756 (audio downloadable)
Subjects: LCSH: Mothers and daughters—Religious aspects—Christianity. | Women—Religious aspects—Christianity. | Bruno, Beth.
Classification: LCC BV4529.18 .B78 2018 | DDC 248.8/431—dc23
LC record available at https://lccn.loc.gov/2017032373

ISBN: 978-1-4789-7465-9 (hardcover), 978-1-4789-7468-0 (ebook), 978-1-4789-7467-3 (trade paperback)

Printed in the United States of America

10 9 8 7 6 5 4 3 2 1

To Ella and Sophie

May you Know you are Wanted,
Valued, Purposed

Contents

Appendices

Introduction

*Do not ask me what I did, ask me what I didn't
do. I did not clip her wings.*
—Ziauddin Yousafzai, Malala's father

I am out to wreck my daughter.

I am out to create a new paradigm of raising girls who
love God, know their voice, and can envision a life of the
two intertwined. To call my teen daughter to something of
these proportions, I need to break her heart the way Jesus'
heart breaks, help her see herself the way He sees her, and
create a framework of womanhood that can hold her as
she develops, doubts, and excels into the future.

There is too much heartache in the world for her voice
to not be heard and too much glory in her soul to not
be unleashed. If I do one parenting thing right, it will be to
raise a young woman who knows her voice is valued, needed,
and essential. I will not relinquish her to the fabricated delay
of childhood called "teenager" and let culture and peers
shape her identity and then expect her to enter adulthood
secure and equipped to make a difference. I believe she is
vital to an epic story and I play a vital role as her mother to
remove the blinders that deceive and seduce her age group.
Casting this vision is my antidote to the teen obsession with
bodies, boys, and besties.

I call it *Becoming*. It is a rites of passage process like no other.

Listening to the messages in teen fiction, movies, music lyrics, and advertising aimed at shaping the next generation, I am not surprised when I see parallel storylines in the teens I am around. "Your value and worth come from being a sex object" plays out in girls' poor body image, clothing choice, and behavior with boys. "To be cool, you need a boyfriend" permeates every young and short-lived romance as our kids stack up heartaches and betrayals. And perhaps worst of all, the belief "Teenage years are for fun, friends, and delayed responsibility" has created a decade of twentysomethings who have failed to launch. They are simply unprepared to navigate adulthood. As a parent, I am unsatisfied with raising children who live such a small story. Not only do I believe young people are capable of more, I believe the journey toward passionate and purposeful adulthood begins in adolescence.

I do not think I'm alone.

Ideologically, I straddle two generations. At the outer edge of Millennials, I find myself an older mother with younger friends who have different perspectives than women my age. My peers and role models who are just ahead of me in parenting herald from Generation X, to which I officially belong. Theirs is a more traditional and defined faith, church expression, and parenting style. The Millennial movement in the evangelical church, or rather outside of it, is one I relate to and live in the tension of. God is no longer in a nice and tidy box. Nor is Scripture, the way we do church, the expression of our worship, or the orthodoxy of our American Christian culture. Today's Christian parents are having conversations about gender identity and same-sex marriage, creation stewardship and the philosophy of short-term missions. We are no longer worried about worship style used in service or as concerned about the differences between dating and courtship.

Given what our children are facing in the culture they are growing up in, the relevancy of these debates is ridiculous. My daughter was in the third grade when we faced a classmate who transitioned from a boy to a girl over summer. We hosted a thirteen-year-old girl in our home for a month who had already been sexually abused in church and raped by a boyfriend. Purity talks take on an entirely new dimension.

Gone are the traditional families and roles that the previous generation esteemed. Our neighbors' homes are run by stay-at-home dads. Friends and family members reverse stereotypical roles because they enjoy it, are good at it, and no longer carry any cultural baggage around it. This isn't a book about the glass ceiling for women, but rather a new approach to raising girls in light of our current culture. I want to usher our daughters into womanhood in a meaningful and intentional way that they can relate to!

This generation of girls will grow up playing with engineering toys such as GoldieBlox and humanly shaped Barbie dolls. They will be in STEM (science, technology, engineering, and mathematics) elementary schools, recruited with an outpouring of engineering and athletic scholarships, and reading magazines that have vowed to not Photoshop their images. Dove and Always ads will change the way they see themselves and define beauty. And they may worship at a church in which women speak and lead and pastor. We almost saw our first female president.

Like it or not, my generation of women has struggled through the mommy wars, the career-versus-stay-at-home dilemma, and all our other identity issues to birth daughters who know with all their heart they were born to bring their gifts to the world in a purposeful and intentional way.

What we tearfully wrestled through, our daughters know innately. They have been born into a culture and to mothers who nurture if not breed it:

They are needed. Wanted. Valued. Purposed.

How then do we usher them through the transition to womanhood?

I interact with teens all the time in my work to prevent human trafficking. Through arts, photography, and leadership development, the organization I direct seeks to empower those most vulnerable to being trafficked to become peer leaders. I listen to these kids and I hear the whisper of culture's influence on their self-worth. Boys are considered cool if they're called a pimp, defining norms for how they behave in relationships. Girls are sleazy if they're called a ho, yet also acutely aware of their sexuality and the power it yields. For many, they have come to believe their value lies in this power. They get caught up in sexting, offer too much too soon in relationships, and are tempted to dance, strip, or more for money. These are my daughters' classmates, friends, youth group buddies. If this is what engulfs our youth, how can books that merely skim the surface of the reality they face adequately help parents?

This generation of girls might enjoy the traditional rites of passage programs many churches offer, but it is not where they will draw meaning. The framework of our girls' sense of femininity places relatively little significance in these events. They have no schema for purity promises and crowning ceremonies. As meaningful as these might have been in previous generations, our girls need more. While they may still hold value, they cannot be the pinnacle of rites of passage for our daughters.

My oldest daughter stands at the edge of womanhood. A teen in middle school, we are discussing the expansion of her hips, the need for a bra, and how to discern when the boys are flirting. She is the middle child and the daughter of a counselor. Her dad is the founder of a nonprofit that architects experiences for men to heal their wounds, know their God, and restore their world. Eradicating fatherlessness is part of their mission that has led to intentional fathering materials, expeditions, and a yearlong rites of passage process for our older son. In essence, our home is saturated with chatter around puberty, adulthood, and intentional experiences for youth.

A few summers ago, we were sunning on our ragged beach towels during a swim break. My fourteen-year-old son sprawled on his back and cradled his head in his hands, armpit hair plainly visible to his shocked sisters, the youngest of whom exclaimed, "Oh my gosh! Aidan!" The siblings had begun watching for little sprouts years prior and had celebrated together when "peach" and "fuzz" burst forth from my son's "pits." With the first noticeable signs of puberty, they continued to openly chronicle his height gain, voice deepening—giggling at his expense when it squeaked—and the new struggle with acne. It had apparently been awhile, though, since they had seen his "pits."

Just as public as his journey through puberty was the rites of passage process my husband orchestrated. Dubbing it the "Man Year," he crafted twelve months of experiential challenges in biblical qualities of masculinity, inviting six men to each spend a few days with our son culminating in a test and a ceremony. The year commenced on his twelfth birthday and involved some pretty incredible opportunities: he sailed in the Pacific and flew in a Cessna with one uncle; he backpacked for four days with a good friend; he flew alone to Florida to be with one of his grandpas; and his dad took him on a ministry trip to the Middle East.

Needless to say, our daughters have been watching. And waiting.

I have an incredible task before me.

What I lack in my own experience (for who among us experienced a rites of passage process as a young teen?), I know this to be true: my daughter is incredibly different than and yet strikingly similar to my son. She is developing physically sooner, maturing in her relationships and inner doubts earlier, and in need of our intentional validation more than my son was at this age. Her passage will look different than our son's rites of passage. Yet she too needs physical challenges and adventure latent with risk. She too longs to be altogether called to a larger story. What draws her most to her brother's Man Year is that he was deemed able. She aches to prove she too has what it takes, that she has the strength needed to be a woman in today's world.

Indeed, it is the very thing I find lacking in many rites of passage books and programs available to moms like me. Special ceremonies and crowns, rings and promises, princess language or retreats with other women are not inherently bad. But I find them deeply lacking. My generation has fought so many battles to create a climate in which our daughters' voices are valued. Now we need to teach them how to use it. Too many rites of passage models re-create the cages from which girls have already been freed. Honestly, I have no desire to create a model at all. I want to create a conversation, a way of thinking, a new paradigm of being rather than another prescription for Christian parents to follow.

Our girls need to be called to something greater. The weight of their femininity is needed in our culture. It is needed in the kingdom of God. His story for His daughters is far larger than we could ever imagine. Why shouldn't we create a space for girls to experience it?

Architecting such a space will take time. The primary goal is not to impart everything my daughter needs to know to be a secure and godly woman (am I?), but to create a scaffolding on which she can hang future doubts and questions, experiences, and successes. As my husband did for our son, I hope to fashion for our daughter a framework of womanhood that honors her *and* God and is sturdy yet flexible enough to remain constant in adulthood. I want to invite her to become, as we are all in the process of becoming more like Christ.

I want to invite her to the company of women, to the art of becoming.

It has taken me forty years to realize the real art of living is messy. There are no scripts we rehearse or play out day by day. No one method of marriage or parenting or ministry is the secret to fulfilled and meaningful living. Fellow believers work out their faith in various and beautiful ways, valuing diverse aspects of God's heart to the neglect of others. And I cannot embrace them all. I fail and adapt. I grow bored and switch things around. I read and am challenged and begin to think differently. We are on a journey, all of us. Not rigid, but flexing as we listen and (hopefully) follow the Spirit's leading. It has taken me decades to realize that life is art. It is sacred and it is participatory. We are cocreators with God in what He has purposed for us to do. If we have eyes to see, it is a messy beautiful process in becoming.

To this I invite you and your daughter. To a paradigm of being, not a prescription for living. Not to a life of obligation, but to one of grace and whimsy. What does a theology, what does femininity, look like full of grace and whimsy? Can we find this together?

Part 1

THE ART OF BECOMING
STARTS WITH MOM

THE ART OF BECOMING
STARTS WITH MOM

1

Beyond Periods and Purity

My first attempt at grace and whimsy was a royal failure. She was far too appreciative of my effort to say so at the time, but weeks later in a moment of exhaustion and sibling rivalry, the truth came out. She DID NOT want her "woman year thing" to look like THAT. Ahem.

I'll be honest. It all seemed daunting. I did not feel nearly creative enough nor did I desire to reinvent wheels that already existed and had worked for some. I had found a series that would provide intentional time with me and Dad while covering some of the issues I believe girls face: beauty, modesty, boys, and friendships. These were topics I deemed appropriate for her eleventh-to-twelfth year, her first year in middle school, the year before the official launch of her rites of passage.

In the early stages of figuring this all out, I welcomed a plan. This offered one so specific I could memorize the script if I wanted! I knew it was girly and planned for it to be a mere launchpad, but I had no idea how badly I would miss my daughter's heart by executing it.

Despite her warnings that she did not want to have a tea party, our inaugural date started at a Victorian teahouse. I was excited. I love tea and scones and all things British. The teahouse was supposed to serve as a live object lesson as we discussed the quality of our words, actions, dress, et cetera.

We dressed up and found an adorable place, but there were all sorts of distractions that mirrored the ways in which I was missing her heart. For instance, she hated the tea, even with lots of sugar and cream. She kept fidgeting with her skirt (the only one she owned), uncomfortable in the forced attire. And we were the youngest and quietest patrons, eventually requesting to move into an empty alcove to hear ourselves above the loud ladies' groups. She felt out of place—not special—on every level.

Had I really thought about my daughter, Ella, I would have known all this. We had never ever played tea party. She owned zero dolls that she dressed up and perched in little chairs around a pink tea set. The only Barbies in our home were mine from childhood. We did have one plastic dollhouse set, but my son played with it more than the girls, knocking dolls off the roof and running cars into the front door. Ella had stopped choosing to wear dresses at the age of three and even at age eleven was uninterested in makeup, hairstyles, and other bling. My daughter is not a girly-girl. Certainly not one to relish the finery of an English tearoom.

Of course, the failure of my first activity might very well be the success of another mom. But that *is* the point. Our daughters are different, yours and mine. Stereotypes have formed that say all girls *should* enjoy what I tried to create for mine: dress-up, pampering with special foods in special places, dainty china as a meaningful metaphor for godly speech and action. We are told all girls ask the fundamental questions: *Am I lovely?* and *Do you see me?*

Archetypes exist to categorize and explain behavior. Tests abound on Facebook these days, assigning just about anything to a personality. I suppose we have a need to feel like we belong to a group with a set of descriptions, something that justifies our feelings and excuses our actions. As parents, perhaps we long for these labels even more. I took comfort in my son throwing the dolls off the roof rather than dressing them or doing their hair. "Boys will be boys" assured me that my son was "normal." But are my girls normal? And what does "normal" even mean?

I have two daughters and they are very, very similar. The youngest prefers to play spy over any other pretend play. She has bags, notebooks, crumpled newspapers full of possible codes, and old keyboards and cell phones, which aid in her spy world. She prefers to read animal mysteries over *American Girl Doll*, *Anne of Green Gables*, or *Little House on the Prairie*. While she loves stuffed animals, her favorites are endangered and wild species that become part of an elaborate fire, earth, water, and air duel.

While an archetype for girls might suggest they are asking, *Am I worth fighting for?* I believe my daughters are asking, *Am I fierce enough?* Instead of *Am I lovely?*, mine are also asking, *Am I strong?* So what do we do if the archetype doesn't fit? How do we embrace the truth that God designed girls and boys differently and that male and female reflect Him uniquely while still validating each child's complex design? Indeed, both sides of the spectrum reflect His image.

For as many parents who are raising girls like mine, there exists an equal amount raising girls who perfectly fit the typical example. The question is how to find the right language to ascribe meaning to our daughters. If the tearoom missed her heart, where would I find it?

Periods and Purity

When my first attempt at intentionality failed miserably, I sought the counsel of other women. I created a survey and heard from women with older daughters, younger girls, and no children at all.

Interestingly, in answers to questions regarding rites of passage, most women assumed I meant the onset of our period. And most could not recall their own mothers addressing this monumental change with them at all. It seems my mom was not alone in her embarrassment around intimate topics. Across the board, each woman thought of either puberty or purity when it came to "rites of passage" conversations. Of those who had celebrated this rite with their girls, all of them described an event or a gift: a weekend at a hotel, a dance, a special ring, et cetera. Only one woman mentioned she thought it was a multiyear process.

I find this interesting. It is true that rites are by nature, events. They signify a ceremonial act or ritual. Rites of passage are markers of before and after: marriage, baptism, graduation, et cetera. When talking about girls, the most natural marker in the transition to womanhood is indeed her period. And in the Christian culture, the most natural ceremonial act between a daughter and her parents has been a purity covenant. I get it. But I'm deeply dissatisfied with it.

Though our society may lack significant rites of passage for girls and boys, they are deeply imbedded in other cultures. The Luiseño Indians of Southern California used to publicly announce their daughters' onset of menses through a ceremonial burial in heated sand. Several girls would go through it at once while the older women of the tribe taught them various things about being a good woman. At one point they ate tobacco as a test of their value: if they swallowed it they were good, if they vomited, they were bad. The sand ritual was followed by several months of various restrictions, the donning of a special headdress, and culminated in the girls painting on large granite boulders, some of which can still be seen today.

In Africa, rites of passage are considered "critical in nation building and identity formation."[1] It is the transition from child to adult that inculcates them to group norms and expectations. For the Twa tribe, girls celebrate their menses (which is considered a blessing) by spending an entire month in a house with elder women instructing them on their history and future roles as a woman, namely being a good wife and mother. When the girl emerges from the home, she is deemed a woman and eligible for marriage.

Though spanning continents and history, most rites of passage have a lot in common. The girl's physical change is celebrated in the community of other women. She is welcomed into the greater company of women, past, present, and future. And she is deemed ready and worthy of her future calling at the passage's conclusion. While they might commence at the onset of menses, they encompass far more personal formation than body change. And yet this is all that we have distilled from these ancient rites of passage traditions: periods and purity.

In our current culture, girls experience a variety of "rites." At some point, younger and younger, they receive a smartphone, opening them to the world of social media pressure and instant online access to videos, photographs, and strangers. Here begins the confirmation of what Disney XD has already taught them: their value is commensurate with trendy fashion, knowing how to dupe parents, and toying with a boy's emotions to get what they want. Inundated with unmitigated advertising "promoting the idea that certain products—not family, community, personal goals, or achievements—will

---

1. Tasha Davis, "African Rites of Passage," accessed on December 2, 2016, http://www.africanholocaust.net/ritesofpassage.html.

lead to being *cool*,"[2] our kids' self-worth is wrongly shaped. If our girls do not receive a counter-story, they will be led to believe they need what culture tells them they need to have any worth at all.

Soon after the rite of the coveted smartphone, she attends her first school dance. With lights off, slow music and awkward coupling encourage her to "date" for the first time, lasting a few days and mostly via social media. As she grows, the expectation to have a more serious boyfriend increases as well as social pressure to lose her virginity. By the time she gets her driver's license and graduates high school, two major rites of passage for modern American teens, most girls will have already come to believe that their value and self-worth come from being a sex object. This is what music lyrics and videos, teen fiction, movies, and commercials have been telling them for years. It is what they saw played out on their phone, in Snapchat and on Instagram, at the school dances, and in the hallways.

In fact, by the time she puts on her cap and gown, 8 percent[3] of her friends have harmed themselves, 9 percent have attempted suicide[4], 64 percent have had sex[5], 7 percent have gotten pregnant[6], and 40 percent of sexually active girls

---

2. Holly Austin Smith, *Walking Prey: How America's Youth Are Vulnerable to Sex Slavery* (New York: Palgrave Macmillan, 2014), 63.

3. Kate Kelland, "One in 12 Teenagers Self Harm, Study Finds," November 17, 2011, http://www.reuters.com/article/2011/11/17/us-self-harm-idUSTRE7AG02520111117.

4. https://www.childtrends.org/indicators/suicidal-teens/.

5. https://www.cdc.gov/mmwr/pdf/ss/ss6304.pdf.

6. Centers for Disease Control and Prevention, "About Teen Pregnancy," http://www.cdc.gov/teenpregnancy/about/index.htm.

have had an STD[7]. If she's not confused about who she is as a woman, many of her peers certainly are. They are careening into college and marriage unclear as to where their value derives, looking to men to affirm them, and deeply insecure. Eventually, married for ten hard years and mothering a few toddlers, they limp into my husband's counseling office unsure how they got there and with little idea how their story has impacted their present reality.

We owe our daughters more than this. And the cure is our intentionality.

Conversations around periods and purity may be a portion of what we impart to our girls, but it cannot be all. They need us to cast a vision of who they are becoming. Why have they been created? What story is being told through their lives? If we succeed at lifting their eyes out of the teen drama of bodies, boys, and besties then we have painted a picture of womanhood that captures them: they know they are needed and valued in God's kingdom, starting right now. They know they are being invited to join a global sisterhood that reflects the image of God.

We need to build a framework of womanhood upon which they can hang all future doubts, experiences, and questions. They need a framework to reference when culture tells them otherwise. Our daughters need a rite of passage that invites them to join the company of women and prepares them to join us. If this sounds at all intimidating, you are in good hands. If you're overwhelmed, you're in good company. So am I. I'm a fellow sojourner, stumbling through this with

---

7. Health and Human Services, Office of Adolescent Health, "Adolescent Development and STDs," accessed December 2, 2016, http://www.hhs .gov/ash/oah/adolescent-health-topics/reproductive-health/stds.html.

you out of deep longing for something more. I believe this is so vital that with God's help and one another, we can change the trajectory of our daughters' lives. Will you join me? I think it's worth it.

I call it *Becoming*.

On Periods

I was twelve and something was happening.

We were a full day's car ride from home and surrounded by all the relatives. My grandparents' house was nestled in a wood with cornfields behind and a mortician living down the lane. The small town felt isolated, stalled, and like their home, frozen in time. The baby-blue toilet with the padded seat cover was my hiding place.

In the kitchen, aunts and uncles, grandparents, and the mortician neighbor enjoyed happy hour. It was Christmas and we were all together. There was no privacy, though I pulled my mother down the hall to the baby-blue bathroom next to the thirteen-inch TV with Miss Piggy sitting atop. I was horrified. My underpants were brown and sticky and I had absolutely no category for this. My mother paused. An embarrassed smile was gone as quickly as I detected it and she brushed it off. "Too much chocolate" she said.

Six months later it was spring and the sticky returned red. Now, from health class I presume, I knew what this was. I knew what to ask for. I knew what was happening. Years later, on the eve of my wedding, when the same smile returned to her face, I recalled the baby-blue toilet. I remembered that at age ten, I had asked what French kissing was and she said she had no idea. I remembered another toilet at age fourteen, from which I received coaching from a friend. She handed me a tampon and mirror and closed the door, not letting me out till I was successful.

And though I managed despite my mother's embarrassment around intimate and feminine topics, what I recall her telling me that Christmas at my grandparents' has framed the bulk of my parenting: There will be no topic too intimate to discuss candidly (and age appropriately) with my kids.

I tried this philosophy out when my son was five. I found him in the bathroom with the contents of the vanity all over the floor. Two-year-old Ella was on the tile floor with eye shadow and lipstick above her eyes, around her lips, and near her ears. Half of her foot was covered in nail polish. Next to her on the floor were several tampons, unwrapped and unrolled. Of course, "What are these, Mommy?" followed.

Here was my chance! Embarrassed smile? Sigh, deep breath? Or just a matter-of-fact straight-faced truthful answer? Oh, Beth, choose well! So I told them. "They are for women to use once a month when they bleed." "Okay," my son said and moved on to the makeup. Not making it a deal made it not a deal. What a relief. And it paved the way for future conversations about all sorts of intimate matters.

So Ella and I have been having body talks for years, whenever her curious mind pops a question. The only way to normalize something is to talk about it frequently and casually. (I address this in more detail in the appendix.) I forced myself to say all the words: vagina, pubic hair, penis, oh my! In fifth grade, I bought her a little coin purse, put some sanitary pads in it, and told her to keep it with her. As the time approached, I gave her more and more specifics.

But when "it happened" (the text I received from Ella), I was out of the country.

In all my determination to handle things differently than my own mother, in the end, it was out of my control. In the greatest irony of all, it was my mom who was with her! Cosmic justice? God's sense of humor? No, in an act full of grace and redemption, my mom was given a second chance.

The process of *Becoming* wrapped her up and carried her along, joining grandmother and granddaughter in a journey of unraveling her narrative and rifling through her own story. Confronted with what she failed to do for me, she grieved what was and embraced what could be with her granddaughter. From across the ocean, I watched this monumental passing in their lives.

There will be no public celebration, but I have tried to muster excitement (Tell me of a woman who actually enjoys this reality! We don't get to spend five days out of the month sequestered in a red tent, like the ancient Israelites, with our friends and sisters after all!).

Rather, we have commemorated that she is joining the ranks of women from all time, from all over. I want her to know that though she'll continue on as a kid who now has pads in her backpack, still getting tucked into bed at night, some of her global sisters are experiencing a radical change of life. At the same age, a young girl in Afghanistan or Yemen is now declared eligible for marriage. A peer in Uganda may stop going to school at this point because she lacks sanitary pads to keep her clean. In fact, when I returned home, our celebration of her first period was to sponsor a year's supply of pads for a Ugandan girl of the same age.[8]

The onset of a girl's period is important for sure. But it will be a mere slice in the process of *Becoming*.

On Purity

I read Elisabeth Elliot's *Passion and Purity* in tenth grade (the Gen X version of *I Kissed Dating Goodbye*), just one year after becoming a Christian. It marked the end to kissing,

---

8. *3 Therapists Walk into a Blog*, "Monumental Moments," blog entry by Beth Bruno, November 9, 2015.

touching, and even dating boys before meeting my husband. It also completely messed me up. Four years later I was falling in love, but frightened of my feelings. They felt wrong. I should be studying and focused on God's call on my life, not interested in this guy, whose every look and comment held me captive. I tortured his poor soul and was fortunate he stuck it out. Eventually, he firmly put his foot down and declared, "I want to date you and call it dating." I was so terrified of the word *dating*. I was so captured by the philosophy of courting, that *I love you* equaled a proposal, and the scary word *dating* should never be used.

I was raised by lovely Christian role models who discipled me in my new faith, picked me up for youth group meetings, and one summer drove me across the country to a conservative Christian leadership camp. I did not get a purity ring or a special purity ceremony, but my friends nurtured the purity principle in convincing ways. By the time my would-be husband said, "I love you," I responded with, "Are you sure you want to say that?" Oh the poor man!

My naive little self continued for years until I started to disciple girls struggling with the purity principle. Girls who were no longer virgins but now new believers. And then, women in my small group who married after they moved in together. Friends who "did things" for previous boyfriends. Respected leaders whose children predate their wedding day. And divorce. And affairs. And pornography addiction. And emotional abuse. And same-sex attraction. All scandalous to purity ears, but all needing grace and love and forgiveness. And all granted such grace by the only one able to give it, God Himself. Who, then, was I to rob them of my love?

When the debates around the purity culture of the last two decades began, my heart was primed. Women began confessing that they harbored guilt and disgust at themselves that they didn't wait. They felt condemned by a church that placed so much stock in their virginity. As if it is *the* prized possession of our faith, the only jewel in the crown worth obtaining. Married women began writing about how it impacted their intimacy; years into marriage they still struggled to feel free, so bound by the prescription of purity.

In a prescription for living, we create lists of rules. We arbitrarily pick ages that certain steps can be taken and define parameters around where, what, and when. The measure of control a daughter has in any situation is bolstered by our strength rather than her inner core and intuition because we have spent far more time focused on the former. Inevitably, the focus of purity centers more around lists and checkoffs, not her heart and relationship with God. As Debra K. Fileta, author of *True Love Dates*, explains, "We spend so much time discussing physical purity, without challenging this generation to live a life that is so Spirit-filled, Christ-centered and God-breathed that purity is just the natural overflow."[9]

Yes, what then would I be teaching my daughters? Do I believe it is best to wait until marriage to consummate your love? Yes. Do I believe the Bible affirms this? Yes. But will I put so much emphasis on it that my girls fear anything on the spectrum of love from being asked on a date to intimacy in the bedroom? I may be wrong, but if she loses her virginity before marriage by choice or force, I don't want her sexual shame to be tied to her parents. I would rather she rest in our love and acceptance. She'll need it. Who else to come to in fear or with the consequences? Who else will hold up the mirror and remind her who she is when she doubts? I don't really want her looking at a symbolic ring, reminding her of

---

9. Debra K. Fileta, "Have We Made an Idol Out of Sexual Purity?" *Relevant*, July 29, 2014, https://relevantmagazine.com/life/relationships/have-we-made-idol-out-sexual-purity.

all her failures and of our disappointment. She'll probably struggle enough with her own shame and her relationship with God.

So, no purity ring. No special ceremony where we essentially make a covenant with her, declaring our partial ownership of her body and choices. Yet, she needs to feel safe and empowered. Children need to know they are protected by boundaries, parents' expectations, and our authority. Equally so, they need to know we can handle their questions and welcome authentic conversation around this subject.

We are painting a picture of a godly, healthy relationship. We not only model this in our own marriage, but openly discuss it as a family. In friendship and dating relationships, we encourage our kids to spend time with someone who values what they value, who honors their opinions by listening to them and asking them questions, who respects their boundaries, who is kind to others and especially their parents, who has goals and is responsible, who loves God by word and action. And we remind them of the design for marriage that we talked about years ago. We go back to God.

Far after she starts her period and walks down the aisle, my daughter will still be asking questions about her femininity. If she is anything like me, she will wrestle with her roles, responsibilities, and relationships for decades. She will question her voice, wondering if it is too much or not enough. She will struggle and doubt and celebrate and marvel at womanhood. And then one day, she will look into the precious porcelain face of her daughter and be thrown for a tailspin once again. We cannot inoculate our daughters from their own journey, but we can prepare them with the arc of a good story.

Let us model our African sisters and Native mamas and truly form our girls into women. Let us transition them to womanhood so that no doubt lingers—they are one of us. Let us cast a vision for who God has designed them to be that far exceeds sexuality and lifts their eyes toward a story worthy of their glory. The world needs them.

Questions for you:

1. What is your story of starting your period? How involved was your mother? How have you determined to do things the same or differently with your daughter as a result?

2. What is your "purity" story? What do you remember being told? How has it impacted you?

3. Do you have unresolved feelings around either of these categories that you need to address before you decide what to share with your daughter?

2

Setting the Stage for *Becoming*

Fellow moms, sisters, if you are anything like me, you have teetered between feeling too much and not enough most of your adult life. You have worn shame. You have fought to find your voice. You have pored through Scripture only to discover Jesus' incredible love and respect and downright adoration of you as a woman. And though you doubted in your youth and thinly hoped as a young adult, now you realize you are wanted, valued, and purposed for His kingdom. Perhaps you are still discovering, still seeking, to find your voice. My hope is that you will learn, alongside your daughter, that we are all on the path of becoming. As you turn to your daughter, it is only natural that you raise her to know she too is wanted, valued, and purposed for His kingdom. Not one day as an adult, but right now as a teen.

Come with me along a journey. Join me on a path of becoming in which we call our daughters to womanhood. Let us boldly and fearlessly, with intentionality, transition our girls to women.

Moms be mindful: This process is as much for you as your daughter. Our story will live on in our children. Whatever messes still reign, doubts linger, and grief survives will weave its way into our parenting in one way or another. Our triumphs and successes often want more airtime and hunt for rebirth in our girls' passions and pursuits. This is reality—not to be feared, but embraced. In God's great wisdom and infinite humor, He has intertwined our stories. But we do need to be aware. We need to have read our own narrative to begin the process of releasing our daughter into hers. Brené Brown writes, "Owning our story and loving ourselves through that process is the bravest thing we'll ever do... We own our stories so we don't spend our lives being defined by them or denying them. And while the journey is long and difficult at times, it is the path to living a more wholehearted life."[10]

As I began the arduous task of planning this year and considering the characteristics or aspects of womanhood I wanted to impart to my daughter, I naturally started with myself. Who am I? What is my story? What of me would I want her to model and what would I rather her forget? What about femininity have I wrestled with all these years and how can I prevent her from wrestling with the same things? What am I *still* wrestling with? I started with the obvious: puberty and periods, boys, besties, bras, and bodies—the persistent questions and conversations that needed to be had. But I knew there was so much more. In fact, I'm so convinced that these alone are inadequate, I've purposefully placed them in the appendix, secondary to the heart of the year of *Becoming*. Plenty of books exist that list the important conversations, questions, and behaviors we should address with our daughters. You can read them. Many are helpful.

And, though I started with my own story, I needed to simultaneously start with hers.

---

10. Brené Brown, *Rising Strong: The Reckoning. The Rumble. The Revolution* (New York: Spiegel & Grau, 2016), 40.

A vision of womanhood needs to exist in her current reality. Only in the context of her experience can she relate to and internalize the framework we build. Imagine a building being constructed within and alongside the metal pipes and planks of a scaffolding. Our daughters are the building, which one day (in heaven) will be fully finished. The scaffolding allows for the building to grow. It is not the foundation. God is. Instead it is the framework that helps shape and sustain the building process. It allows freedom and flexibility for our daughters to define, reshape, and embellish throughout their own lives.

Creating Mental File Folders

Fully appreciating the longevity of this endeavor, my husband and I sought to create mental file folders for our kids' rites of passage. We know, as Ann Voskamp has articulated, "Oak trees don't happen overnight. Growing in grace and wisdom and stature isn't an immediate download—it happens the way a tree grows up: over decades."[11] I have no expectation that our daughters will pass through this year and be women on the other side, mature beyond their years and peers. But I do hope that they will have the file folders to cross-reference, digest, and categorize future experiences and questions.

One of the qualities of a man that my son learned about during his rites of passage year is "Excellent Action." My husband wanted to call him out of apathy and toward action, to be like men who, as he writes in *Man Maker Project*, "co-labor with God to bring about the restoration of the World." This

---

11. Ann Voskamp, "Help for Mothers Who Want to Give Up: 10 Keys to Raising This Generation of Boys into #GoodYoungMen," May 5, 2015, http://annvoskamp.com/2015/05/how-to-raise-this-generation-of-boys -into-good-young-men-10-keys-to-raising-goodyoungmen/.

provided opportunity to discuss doing homework, cleaning his room, or treating his sisters with excellent action, not half-hearted effort. However, when he turned thirteen and completed the Man Year, my son did not magically become a responsible teenager who never again left his socks around the house or shoved candy wrappers in between couch cushions. What *did* change is how I parent him. By creating the mental file folder of Excellent Action, all I need to do is quietly ask if he believes he did the chore excellently, and off he goes to improve his work. He has a category of what we expect, of what God honors, and of who he needs to become as a man during these fits and jolts of shedding the boy.

For my daughter's *Becoming* year, I chose five ways in which I believe women reflect the image of God. I believe these transcend time and culture, for if they are truly a reflection of God in us, then they should be true of women from five hundred years ago as well as women who are Iranian or Canadian today. The five categories I chose are: *women lead, women love, women fight, women sacrifice,* and *women create.* I have seen these to be true of women in Scripture, of women throughout history, and in my own life. But I believe there are many more and they will vary based on the unique personality and passion of each mom and daughter. The important thing is that we cast a vision for who our daughters can become. In lifting their eyes to the bigger story that God is writing, we call them to offer the fullness of who they are to the kingdom of God. I believe this is the way we shift their obsession from bodies, boys, and besties to a life worthy of their glory.

Paradigm of Being vs. Prescription for Living

I've already mentioned wanting to create a paradigm of being versus a prescription for living. What do I mean by that?

Like the purity movement, which created a list of rules and restrictions, a good chunk of evangelicalism has left a legacy of *how* to be a believer. As an evangelical baby, I am still untangling myself from some of the things on the list: how to have a quiet time, how to pray, how to share your faith, how to date, how to parent, how to educate your children, how to be a wife and a mom, how to please your husband, and on and on.

Addie Zierman processes some of these on her blog, *How to Talk Evangelical* and in her memoir, *When We Were on Fire*. She tells the story of her RA at Bible college asking how her "walk" was: "I wanted her to *see* that I had been a Bible Study leader. I wanted her to *see* me anointing the Prayer Table at school. I wanted her to feel what I felt, to understand that I had been fighting so long to prove myself and I was tired."[12] How many of us moms of teens grew up doing it all and have grown tired? I wonder if much of the church-abuse counseling, church splits, and social-media derision come from the tension of living this prescriptive life.

I'm done living by prescription. It is suffocating our faith and limiting God. I've talked to too many women who like me went into full-time ministry because it was the highest calling in the evangelical world and returned to "normal life" wracked with guilt and without a sense of their value and purpose. Too many women are paralyzed by making the best choice for their children's schooling and live fearing it's the wrong one according to their church culture. Too many women believe the only way to relate to God is by doing a thirty-minute devotional each morning or studying the Bible with a certain method. I was that woman. I lived

---

12. Addie Zierman, *When We Were on Fire* (New York, NY: Convergent Books, 2013), 111.

a prescriptive life and my faith suffered—my view of God grew smaller and smaller.

I want to call my daughter to a theology of grace and whimsy. If there are boundaries, they are to seek God, to be filled with His Spirit, and to live by Scripture. Emily Freeman, who creates a space for souls to breathe, explains, "We don't have to be so afraid of desire. It's time instead to wake up to it. In the waking, maybe we will begin to see that instead of principles to follow, life is more like a rhythm to move with."[13] A paradigm of being is a generous lens that elevates God to being so big we can't fully understand Him and yet small enough to intimately know us, a generous lens that accepts our own limitations of knowledge and Christian living, and worries more about loving and serving others than getting it right. If our daughters are to be prepared to live in a world of shifting values and increasing pain, they'll need this sort of lens. They'll need to learn that life is a rhythm to move with more than parameters to live within. A paradigm of being frees her to follow Jesus into the future, not just the present.

The Role of Other Women

If we're allowed a request in heaven, I am prepared. I have long dreamed of a fire pit on a warm summer night, crickets in the background, and someone tapping a beat on a small drum. A circle of women is gathered to share stories. Miraculously, we all share a common tongue. It is what happens in heaven, when a translation app is programmed into our brains. We are a vibrant group of colors, in both skin and clothing. We herald from the span of history and the breadth of the world, but we are connected. Heaven has taught us

13. Emily P. Freeman, *A Million Little Ways* (Grand Rapids, MI: Revel, 2013), 67.

how similar we are, though life in the twenty-first century has flattened our exposure to each other. The newest additions to this heavenly fire pit, like myself, have already befriended women across oceans via Facebook and begun reading and learning from their experiences. A woman with a headdress stands up and in a singsong spoken-word kind of way, begins to talk about her daughter. We all nod in deep felt agreement. For when it comes to raising girls to reflect the glory of God, culture, language, and time are transcended.

Of course, I would prefer to experience this before I get to heaven. Because the beauty of women reflecting God is everywhere. And it is to this we invite our daughters: to a global sisterhood. If we are to welcome our daughters to join the company of women, they must know they are a part of an incredible history and a beautiful cast of characters. At the end of this rites of passage year, our girls need to know the story they are joining. This means including key women in our lives to join us in the journey, in addition to women of history and women of the world. I wanted my daughter to interact with Turkish women, whom I hold with such high esteem. I wanted her to read stories of women in other countries and find heroes from various cultures. We are raising global daughters. We are also raising daughters who embrace God's design for women. They need to see universal truths, not only the specific application of femininity in America.

Honestly, I want to break my daughter's heart for that which breaks God's heart. It is the plight of American middle-class girls to worry about their Snapchat story and Instagram selfie. Syrian refugee girls are worried about becoming a child bride. To what do we owe our sisters around the world? If I can raise Ella to see her place in the world as a part of a glorious whole, rather than the center of a world of her making, then I'm setting her up to have the kind of humility that will really bring change.

It's one thing to curate stories of global women, past and present, to read their stories and watch the films. We all have a list of heroines we can introduce our girls to, some in person, but mostly through story. We also have lots of "in real life" women who are special friends and family who join us in the journey. Many of my women have their own daughters and are watching and waiting. We talk at length about *Becoming*. They have helped shape my thinking and have been a wise sounding board. While my daughter knows I care for them all, I want her to experience them as a fellow woman. As I invite her into the company of women, it is important for her to experience them as more of a peer and not merely a child. I need their help in transitioning her from girlhood. And, I need her to hear and learn from them if for no other reason as my reinforcement crew.

The Role of Dad

As important as other women are to the process of *Becoming*, we cannot neglect the role of Dad. Intentional fathering is critical to the health of the family, the children, and indeed all of society. My husband, Chris, wrote, "Fathers who intentionally turn their hearts toward their children change the course of history, not only for that child, but for the world. Consider the final verse of the Old Testament in Malachi 4:6, God's last prophetic words about Christ before four hundred years of bleak silence: 'He will turn the hearts of the fathers to their children, and the hearts of the children to their fathers; or else I will come and strike the land with a curse.' "[14]

Chris explains the results of America's fatherlessness

14. Chris Bruno, *Man Maker Project: Boys Are Born, Men Are Made* (Eugene, OR: Resource Publications, 2014), 113.

epidemic: an increase in poverty, incarceration, teen pregnancy, child abuse, substance abuse, obesity, and poor school performance in fatherless homes. He says, "In essence, the welfare of society rests on the intentions of fathers. 'Father well,' God says, 'and the world is blessed. Father poorly, and the world crumbles. It's really that big.'"

When my husband began designing our son's Man Year, he drew from a depth of resources, multiple organizations, and his own client notes to show the results of uninitiated boys. The outcomes are dire. If boys are not intentionally ushered into manhood, they can become dangerous to society. My husband knew this responsibility fell on him to initiate our son: "If they do not receive this from the father, they look to false fathers such as gangs, drugs, workaholism, sex, pornography, sports, or anything that may come close to affirming their manhood."[15] Boys become men through other men.

As leaders in domestic anti–sex trafficking, my husband and I have a working theory on the role of fatherlessness in the exploitation of girls and the demand for sex from male buyers. If the failure to make men of boys rests on the father, then the absence of this initiation leaves boys with unfinished masculinity. Too often they prove their manhood through aggression, pornography, and other paths that can lead a boy to becoming a buyer of sex. On the flip side, when girls are not intentionally fathered into womanhood, they become vulnerable. When girls doubt their femininity, they are more easily exploited by those providing answers. Our daughters' generation is oversexualized, bombarded by cultural messaging that tells them their value and worth come from being a sex object. Without a counter message and without a strong sense of their female self that is imparted by engaged and

---

15. Ibid., 8.

loving parents, too many girls find what they long to hear from traffickers and exploitative men. The role of the father is really that big.

During our son's Man Year, I played a very small role, as one of the atmospheric conditions boys need to become men is removal from the feminine. But for our daughter's year, we believed just the opposite was essential. Dad had to be involved. While I led the process, my husband had several intentional experiences and conversations with her based on passions they share. The transition from girl-child to young woman can be an awkward season for fathers. Right before their eyes, their little girl changes into a little woman, but her craving for physical affection, romping, and approval remains the same. Dads have to affirm their daughters' desire for touch, affirmation, and individualized attention. Dr. Meg Meeker, in her widely read *Strong Fathers, Strong Daughters*, admonishes dads, "Spending time with your daughter shouldn't be full of pressure, because she doesn't need you to *do* anything; she only needs to be with you. All she wants is your attention. And she needs it on a regular basis."[16]

Of course, there are plenty of blended family homes and single moms reading this book. If dad is absent or in a strained relationship with you or your daughter, or if another man plays a more significant role in your family, then reality dictates an alternate course. Stepfathers, grandfathers, close uncles, and friends whom you know and trust can all step in to fill some of the vital needs a girl has for a father figure. Even healthy interactions with teachers, coaches, and youth group leaders can positively shape a girl's sense of self and understanding of men and craft pathways of healthy interactions with the opposite sex. But moms, let me encourage

16. Meg Meeker, *Strong Fathers, Strong Daughters: 10 Secrets Every Father Should Know* (New York: Ballantine, 2006), 57.

you to not shield her from men, even if you have suffered because of them. Too often, women who carry wounds from their own fathers or who have been betrayed, abandoned, or harmed by their husband allow their pain to seep into their daughter's perception of men. Hold out hope for her story to be different and trust that not all men are so wounded that all they can do is harm. Chances are, the men who hurt you lacked strong fathers themselves. Be a legacy breaker and dare to give your daughter a different narrative. Value the role fathering plays in her process of *Becoming*.

A Peek at the Plan

In part two, you will read about the rites of passage year I designed for my daughter. After our launch, we worked through five categories: *women lead, women love, women fight, women sacrifice,* and *women create*. They are meant to inspire you, as you may decide on very different categories. Each chapter contains not only questions for you to engage your own story but also two simple charts: the one I created and a blank one for you to use. I also included stories from other women I have grown to deeply respect. Their stories illustrate how we can be unique as we raise strong girls into women.

The yearlong process is intentional. I don't know about your kids, but mine have a twenty-minute attention span for deep conversation. I knew that for anything to really sink in, the topic needed to be ingested through videos, books, activities, and conversation peppered along the way. Over the course of a year, I spent about eight weeks on each category with some flexibility around the holidays. While I had been thinking and planning for years and sketched a blueprint, I was awed by how God brought things along the way. Documentaries, events, and books were released just when

I needed them and fit in perfectly to what we were doing. I am an odd mix of a planner and a spontaneous nonplanner, and it worked out beautifully!

We framed the year with God's two questions to Hagar:

- *Where have you come from?* as a launch to firmly ground Ella in our family story.
- *Where are you going?* as a conclusion to ground her in God's story.

We will cover this more thoroughly, but know that both the launch and conclusion should be special. These two events mark the intentional year you are dedicating to *Becoming*. They prepare your daughter to begin the process and to know when it is completed. All rites of passage include a "test" at the end that determines she is ready to enter the company of women. I'll show you what I did, but know that myriad creative ideas exist. I cannot wait to hear what you come up with for your daughters!

In the appendix, you will find a host of resources to start your journey: ideas on how to fund this year (I guarantee you can make this year special for your daughter within any budget; I had to get very creative to fund my ideas); resources for books, movies, activities, and so forth that you might find better suited to your daughter than what I chose; and blank charts to start working on your plan.

Just remember: My aim is to offer a framework for the year, not a specific program to follow.

Within a process of transitioning our girls into women who offer the fullness of themselves to the kingdom of God, there is room for all of us. There is space at the table for the girly-girls and the athletic girls, for the moms who work full time and the ones who work from home and the ones who work primarily as a homemaker, for those who served as missionaries and take a trip back and those who spend a weekend camping and those who see their first opera because their daughter loves music. Do you hear what I'm saying? What I offer you here is a process, not a program.

One last thing, moms. Are you ready to engage your own story? We can take others only as far as we ourselves have gone. Have you processed the places you feel wounded? Weak? Weary? Are you aware of how your own insecurities hover in conversations with your daughter? Do you realize that your own narrative will be present in the categories you create for her? And are you okay with still being in process?

As we create a scaffolding of womanhood for *Becoming*, we must embrace our own stage in the journey. We are building a framework upon which our daughters will hang future doubts, questions, and experiences. It grows and expands but is stable enough to handle the construction and deconstruction life brings. Women, are you able to do the same? Can you accept that you too are in the process of *Becoming*? It is an art, expressed in myriad ways in our lives. Will you live into that?

Before we begin, I want to tell you more about the global sisterhood we are inviting our daughters to join as well as explain how God's questions to Hagar frame the rites of passage year.

Questions for you:

1. What are some of the first categories of womanhood that come to mind? Meaning, in what ways do *you* think women reflect the image of God? Why do you think these popped into your head immediately?

2. Who are some of the women in your real life that you would want to include in your daughter's *Becoming* year?

3. Where is her dad in your life? If he's not around, who are the men who fill that role for your daughter? If there isn't one yet, who might you begin to pursue for that purpose? How might he be involved in this process? Check out the appendix for a section for dads and men written by my husband.

3

An Invitation to a Global Sisterhood

Modesty aside, one of my favorite places is the Çemberlitaş Hamamı (Turkish bath) in Istanbul. Built in 1584 by Mimar Sinan, a famous architect for the Ottoman Empire, it is still used as a bath today. Its ceilings are vaulted with small glass holes that allow light to penetrate and bathe the entire room with its beams. Each room is floor to ceiling marble, a steamy echoing chamber with alcoves lined with brass faucets and marble basins. Even the women who scrub and massage the patrons seem ancient and original.

For centuries, women have found rest, sisterhood, and even celebration among this marble and steam. They have lingered far from household responsibilities, as a retreat from their lives. They have congregated here to eat and dance into long nights. Bridal parties still come to celebrate an upcoming wedding. And it has all been done in the flesh.

Oh yes, the hamam is an experience in immodesty. It is a space where the female body is embraced, where flesh and rolls and scars and moles are plainly visible. It points to a sisterhood that knows how to laugh and accept and enjoy each other without shame. It was a place I wanted Ella to experience.

We are raising women. Not American women. Not twenty-first-century middle-class suburban women, but global women. If we believe God created us in His image, then there must be intrinsic and inherent aspects to women that span cultures, generations, and all other forms of diversity. To mine for these treasures, we must immerse ourselves in their stories.

We've come from a rich and complex tapestry of women that is so beautiful, so diverse, so delightful, and so tortured that I am overwhelmed. History books are not on our side and I am playing catch up to learn about my sisters through the centuries, to read with a feminine lens. What I know is that this rites of passage process needs to invite her to the greater company of women, past and present, to a story of epic proportions worthy of our daughters.

In the next chapter, I will share more of my story, of the Bruno family story and how it is rooted in Turkey. For now, I would like for you to consider the weight of what I'm saying. You are a part of an epic story, a story God has been writing through women and with women and for women throughout the ages and throughout the world. To embrace this is the beginning of creating an intentional rites of passage for your daughter. You have to know what you are calling her toward. God wants her in all the ways he wanted Hagar, Rahab, Mary, Joan of Arc, Corrie ten Boom and Mother Teresa.

Your challenge is to immerse yourself in their stories. This may include trips to a museum, research in the stacks of the local campus library, job shadowing with cool women in your community, Skype calls to missionaries and the people they serve, and lots and lots of books and movies. Stories abound, for we are storied women. Mine led us back to Turkey.

Storied Women

The Çemberlitaş Hamamı is near the Grand Bazaar, whose ceramic red roof tiles have been made famous as of late by Hollywood film crews. I recall Tom Cruise running over them recently. But as any local knows, the real gems are found in the winding alleys that twist and turn down toward the New Mosque (built in 1597) and the Egyptian Spice Bazaar. Here you can find the beads that Turkish women transform into ornate jewelry, antique copper treasures, rare Ottoman books, and of course, the oldest Turkish delight shop.

Perhaps more than any other category of womanhood, the one we most desire is faith. We aspire to be women of faith and want the same for our daughters. And what a rich tapestry of faith-filled women exists! We've come from strong and courageous sisters who have been listening to the small still voice of God throughout time. Their love for Him has outweighed all the other voices seeking to distract, persuade, and lure away. In the streets teeming with covered Muslim women and the call to prayer echoing from the hundreds of minarets piercing the skyline, it feels poignant. Unlike suburban America, whose sights and sounds mask the luring voices rather than assault the senses, there is no pretending in the Middle East. Turkish women of Christian faith have made a distinct and fateful choice among the 99.9 percent Muslim population. And Jesus is the winner.

From the very beginning of *Becoming*, I wove stories of women into our every conversation. We are casting a vision, remember, of who our daughter is joining. For our launch trip, which I'll describe more in the next chapter, I gave my daughter letters each day to craft meaning and name those things I wanted her to internalize. It was a lofty goal, but if we do not name them, the world will name them for us.

Day One of Launch Trip

Dear Ella,

What a day! I know we're tired with jet lag and the brutality of walking on cobblestones. Let's enjoy this dinner and the evening ferry ride back to the Asian side. You know I'm in my glory, right? I'm showing you anew the places I hold so dear. I hope you forgive my walks down memory lane.

Speaking of lanes, I want to talk about the Egyptian Spice Bazaar. Crazy, right? Men calling at us from all sides, beckoning us to try their Turkish delight, to buy their exotic teas. Can you believe the number of options of teas and spices? The colors? The smells? The tastes? Were your senses on overload?

And I wonder at the parallels of your current life and the next few years.

Many choices. Multiple voices.

Whose voice will win? Is it the one who is loudest? The one who is craziest? The one who flatters you the most? (Pretty woman with her lovely daughter! I'll give ten camels for her hand in marriage!)

Which choice will you make? The prettiest? The one that looks most unique? The one that looks safest and most familiar? The one that costs least?

Ella, you are going to be presented with a plethora of options in life and you have already experienced some at school. Will you be all about boys and "dating" because everyone else is? Will you wear makeup and buy certain brands because everyone else does? How will you choose what is important to you and a reflection of you in the midst of everyone around you yelling louder: Do this to be cool!

We are in a land of Muslims. 99.9 percent are Muslim. So when a Turk decides to follow Jesus, they are listening to a small, still voice of God, asking for their faith. They are turning away from the loud, familiar, common voices they have known all their lives. It is risky and some have died for it. They are my heroes. With courage, they have faced rejection at home, bullying at work, and persecution all around to follow the one in whom they have fallen in love, whom they believe is true.

What do you believe is true? Whom will you follow? What small, still voice asks for your faith? That is the voice you need to hear in the midst of all the others. Be brave, my daughter. We've come from a strong and courageous body of believers.

A few days after the Egyptian Spice Bazaar, I handed Ella another letter. It was toward the end of a day I had been dreaming about for eight years. I knew my heart would be pulsing. So much had changed in my own story since I last took in this view. Through a long and tender process, God had shown me that strength and courage are as lovely to him as weakness.

Day Three of Launch Trip

Dear Ella,

I have been waiting for this view for years. Is it familiar? It stares down at us from the ledge above our piano at home. This tower was built in 1348 and was the tallest building in the city at the time. Its name means 'Tower of Christ' in Latin.

As I think about our day and the footsteps we have followed, I am struck by the stories we have encountered.

We started at the hospital in which Florence Nightingale transformed modern medicine and saved hundreds of lives. Compelled by her faith to do something meaningful for the service of others, she left the comfort and expectations of high society in England to take care of soldiers during the Crimean War. What determination!

In Çengelköy, we walked the streets of the neighborhood you remember best; saw the house and the park and the little market that held your early days. The winding staircases and cobblestone streets in which you passed the hours with your beloved babysitter, Zeynep. She was God's gift to our family and eased my mind every time I left you with her. But did you know back then how strong her faith is, how much she loves Jesus, how secure and confident she is as a Turkish woman? I can't wait for you to see her!

And now, here we are in the Tower of Christ, looking out across the Bosphorus to Florence Nightingale's place of ministry. Beneath and around us are streets full of other women. They are my ministry. Exploited women. Women who have stories of hard. Who have been harmed and are harmed still, used and shamed by men. Were we to wander down any alley, we would walk their footsteps.

Ella, I want you to know you've come from determined women. Women of faith. Women of strength and courage and sacrifice, but ours is a story of pain as well. Jesus comes from Rahab the prostitute. He spends time with the woman at the well, living with a man not her husband. He spares another woman her life by casting light on the sin of those who would accuse and stone her. They are His ministry.

And He loves us all.

We are sisters. Throughout time, past, present, and future. Those who are deemed heroines and those

*we call exploited. Women of God. As you begin to
enter our company, never lose sight of the view from
this tower—across the sea to courage and beneath
your feet toward need.*

I had changed since last I climbed Galata Tower. My
faith had changed. And the things that break my heart had
changed. The old Beth had had one view: across the sea
toward courage. I saw Rahab, the woman at the well, and
the adulteress as courageous women. I believed Jesus loved
that about them. I didn't understand need then. I couldn't
see what was beneath my feet. Indeed, I had no idea back
then that the narrow streets below Galata Tower were places
of sexual exploitation, that there were legalized and government monitored red-light districts just down the alleyways.

One of the turning points for me in my story was a song
arrangement from Henri Nouwen's *Life of the Beloved*: "You
are broken, I am broken, Everyone is Broken. Bless, bless and
do not curse. For I never realized, broken glass can shine
so brightly." Embracing my own brokenness, weakness, and
need was a long slow process for me. But it was my entry
point to seeing others' needs as beautiful, to understanding
how strength and weakness can coexist. I finally understood
how similar we all are, that we are all sisters.

That's the storyline our daughters join.

A Sisterhood

If we're all sisters, Turks and Americans alike, from ages past
and into the future, what does that mean? If we are inviting
our daughters to an epic story worthy of their calling, what
are we asking of them?

We need to locate them in the storyline of femininity.
They need to hear the stories of our heroines, the legends,

and the cultural icons so they might imagine following in their footsteps. But right alongside of strength and courage, they need to see failure, struggle, and ongoing pain. Plenty of heroines suffered unwanted singleness, illness, rejection, and the consequences of flawed decisions. Plenty more have been persecuted, attacked, and killed for standing up for what they believe in. *Across the sea to courage and beneath your feet toward need.*

To call our daughters to embrace their sisters around the world requires we cast a vision for how to use our privilege to benefit others. In far too many places of the world, gender inequity keeps girls uneducated, improperly fed, or wedded and parenting at young ages. The ripple effect is complicated. As an example, highly patriarchal societies that value boys over girls, result in females receiving leftover food, devoid of milk, meat, and other essential nutrients. Remove balanced nutrition from an entire segment of society (i.e., girls) and the result is lower IQs, less productivity, and a collective decrease in intelligence of their country.

In too much of the world, violence, lack of feminine hygiene products, school supply costs, and cultural values prevent girls from even receiving an education. Early American education activist Anna Dickinson said, "Give to every child in America a spelling book and a free schoolroom, and to every intelligent and respectable person, black and white, man and woman, a ballot and freedom of government, and you will see that this country will stand stronger and stronger amidst the ruins of dissolving empires and falling thrones."[17] How true this has been! Free and compulsory education, the right to vote for all Americans over eighteen, and democracy have been the bedrock of the last century of our great and

---

17. Michelle Roehm McCann and Amelie Welden, *Girls Who Rocked the World* (New York: Aladdin/Beyond Words, 2012), 80.

prosperous nation. I wonder how many of our daughters realize they live in this global discrepancy?

The way our girls are raised, planning their birthday parties and dreaming of a future that includes a family, but not to the exclusion of college and career, is so markedly different! You have to know your birth date to plan a party after all. You have to see women treated with value and respect, or working outside of the home to imagine such a thing. Girl power is an incredibly Americentric aspiration in light of the reality of our global sisters.

And how long has this even been true in the West? What we have now is on the backs of all those who have fought before us. American women won the right to vote only in 1920 (British in 1928, French in 1944, and South Africans in 1994). They left a legacy we women now enjoy. But we are also leaving legacies. What will we write? What will we change now for future generations?

What will wreck our daughters? Will it be food scarcity? Child brides? Perhaps it will be needless deaths from poor maternal health care or lack of immunizations or malaria mosquito nets. Maybe it will be girls' education or the barrier of school supply fees. Will it be orphans? Secure housing? Displaced persons and refugees? Domestic violence and child abuse? Ecology and conservation? What aspect of Jesus' heart will break hers as she learns to collaborate with Him to bring His kingdom to earth as it is in heaven?

What I know is this: Every great story involves an unlikely hero who discovers their strength and glory and finally lives into who they were created to be. God has been telling the same story since the beginning of time. And we are the unlikely men and women, girls and boys who were created for a glory many of us never discover. We are asking our daughters to live out who they were made to be by recognizing that they are a part of something bigger. We're not telling them they are the center of the plot (although that is what most teenagers think). We're not pumping them full of self-empowering ideas of changing the world for the sake of fame and fortune (the direction of many youth enterprises, which lack humility). And we're certainly not saying it is our job as Americans to go save those girls in other countries (unlike far too many missions trips would have her believe).

We are raising our girls to humbly embrace their role in the greater family of God, to consider the ways in which they can share their portion and offer themselves alongside of what God is already doing around the world. There are strong and visionary women in every culture who could effectively lead their generation and their country in ways more reflective of God's kingdom. The question is what do they need from us and how might we assist them?

I knew some of these women and counted them as friends. They are our sisters. What a privilege to see them again with Ella at my side. Who do you know? Who do you need to get to know? How can you journey with your daughter to fully embrace the storyline of femininity and welcome her into the company of women? As you prepare to launch a yearlong rites of passage, consider the women you will introduce her to and the ones whom you will invite her to join. My hope is that you will find traces of strength and purpose and remnants of God's glory.

Day Five of Launch Trip

Dear Ella,

If there was a reason we stayed for seven years, this is it. Today. The people and their faith. We might have originally felt compelled to go to Turkey because of

*the adventure and the principle of such a huge num-
ber of people not knowing Christ, but we stayed
because they stopped being numbers. When they
became our friends and family, love kept us here.*

*Today you've worshipped in a Turkish church. A
little building tucked away from the busy business
street, full of people who love God desperately and
love one another just as deeply. They have chosen
to be different. Countercultural. A tiny minority in a
land that values sameness. Think Jonas in* The Giver.

*You've spent time with friends. These dear people
filled the roles of grandparent, sister and brother,
aunt and uncle. When blood relatives were far, we
became surrogate family to one another. And when
distance separated us, they remained part of our
heart. I hope you saw that today.*

Where have you come from, Ella?

*You've come from rich relationships and stellar
examples of people who sacrifice, serve, and suffer
for the love of Jesus. Don't misunderstand, this can
look different and be lived out anywhere in the world
in any career. The key is that they have identified an
aspect of Jesus' heart that breaks their heart and they
are collaborating with Him to bring the kingdom to
earth as it is in heaven.*

*You're only beginning this journey, Ella. We'll
talk more about God's second question to Hagar—
"Where are you going?"—in a few months. But know
this: You were born into a legacy of strength. Today
you spent time with some of them. They are strong of
character. Strong in purpose. Strong in vision. Strong
in stamina. Strong in faith.*

*Sometimes, in the American way of life, I think
we can be distracted. But here, here we see more*

clearly. And today, I hope you have seen clearly that beautiful, lovely, incredible people welcomed you into this world and have watched you since.

It's what family does. It's what love looks like.

Questions for you:

1. Who are your heroines you want to share with your daughter? Think of women in history, women of our faith, and even strong women you admire today. What about these women inspire you?

2. Do you have the perspective that you are a part of a bigger sisterhood? Do you believe God is telling a similar story through women throughout time and across cultures?

3. What are some ways that you can help your daughter experience this epic story? Are there places to visit, events to attend, Skype calls to arrange?

4. Have you identified an aspect of Jesus' heart that breaks your heart? How are you collaborating with Him to bring the kingdom to earth as it is in heaven? Have you noticed any clues as to what this may be for your daughter?

4

Where Have You Come From?

We are called to reveal God through the themes and dreams he has woven into our heart. Therefore, to know our calling, we must come to name the unique trajectory of our story.

—Dan Allender[18]

For twelve years she has heard the story.

On this day [however many years ago], I awoke knowing you would be born. My water broke in the morning, but just like your older brother, was not accompanied by contractions. Only a clock that began ticking down the hours: twenty-four hours of safety before they would forcibly remove you from my womb. I got to work planting flowers in plastic hanging beds and took a long walk along the water. We were in Moda, Turkey, the house with the terrace that overlooked ancient Constantinople, with

---

18. Dan Allender, *To Be Told* (Colorado Springs, Water Brook Press, 2005), 103.

the cobblestone walkway along the Marmara Sea. It was April twenty-ninth and spring breezes wafted in fish smells. I paused every few feet as contractions were beginning, leaned into your dad's arms.

When we returned to the flat I lay down to rest, but you were coming. Fast. It must have been early evening because traffic was bad and the only route out of our neighborhood took us through the largest street bazaar in the entire country. Through the throngs of people gathering their week's produce before the farmers packed up, the car bumped and pushed and we beeped. Did they see me groaning in agony? I was feeling the urge to push now.

The ER staff seemed doubtful when Dad said "Get a wheelchair!" Most Turkish women schedule a C-section and we wondered how often they had seen natural birth. The next moments were a blur, but within thirty I was holding you. 7:25 p.m.

Your hair was dark and curly and you looked Turkish! Neighbors loved that you were healthy and "tombul" and pinched your cheek and exclaimed, "Maşallah," to ward off evil that would come from envious thoughts. They pinned the nazar talisman to your clothing to protect you from greedy eyes. We tried to be cultural and remain indoors for forty days, but with a three-year-old brother it was impossible. You saw the city before most, different from the very beginning.

The story of any girl's *Becoming* begins with her entry into the family, whether or not she is raised by her birth parents. It is the first tale that anchors her in a bigger narrative arc. She has entered the plot. She is now on the scene: be it via a birth canal, caesarean section, or transatlantic adoption. The details of her "birth" however, are not as important as the storyline she joins. Ella's younger sister was born at Martha Jefferson Hospital in Charlottesville, Virginia, a place we stayed for two months on furlough with our mission agency. Her ache to see the downtown streets I walked waiting for contractions do not rival her ache to see the cobblestone streets I speak so fondly of in the place she returned to after Virginia. She knows the Bruno storyline into which she was born is rooted in Istanbul. It is here that the questions begin, and lie unanswered.

In *The Healing Power of Stories*, Daniel Taylor surmises that "stories go somewhere to roost, somewhere deep inside our spirits. They settle there, beyond consciousness, to grow, blend with other stories and experiences, and work their influence from below, subject only to the distant call of memory." And yet they shape us, inform our present, and haunt our future course. "Within the movement of story and the act of storytelling reside the best answers we have to life's perennial questions: Who am I? Where did I come from? Why am I here? Who are you? What will happen to us when we die?"[19] We are a storied people. God made it so. He located us in the story he is telling and calls us to answer, "Where have you come from?"

This is an ancient question. And the answer we discover is everything. Richard Rohr says, "When you get your, 'Who am I?' question right, all of your, 'What should I do?' questions tend to take care of themselves."[20] In the process of

---

19. Daniel Taylor, *The Healing Power of Stories* (New York: Doubleday, 1996), 11, 5.
20. Richard Rohr, *Falling Upward: A Spirituality for the Two Halves of Life* (San Francisco: Jossey-Bass, 2011).

Becoming, we must firmly ground our daughters in their family story if we hope for them to discover their place in God's story. From where have they come?

God first asks this of His people when He appeared to a frazzled woman on a desert road. Hagar. Abused, with child, on the run, and thirsty, the Lord finds her by a spring of water and dares to ask, "Where have you come from and where are you going?" These questions make my heart stop. Here is a woman whose interaction with God not only perfectly frames our daughters' rites of passage year, but challenges us moms with soul questions to ponder.

We first meet Hagar, the Egyptian maidservant of Sarai, when she is handed over to Abram to conceive a child on Sarai's behalf.[21] We can only assume she came to their household while they were in Egypt. Abram and Sarai had spent an unspecified amount of time there during a famine and some pretty bizarre things occurred. Upon entering the city, Abram told Sarai to pretend she was his sister so Pharaoh would spare his life. He basically traded his wife for his life and an abundance of livestock and servants in return. In fact, Abram was so wealthy by the time they left Egypt that he and his nephew, Lot, could not inhabit the same land and had to part ways. Pharaoh indeed thought Sarai was beautiful and took her to be his wife until God brought disease upon his household. In today's culture, we call this commercial sexual exploitation.

At this point, it is unclear how Hagar comes to their household. Some scholars speculate she was Pharaoh's daughter and that he was so fearful of Abram's god he gifted Hagar to Sarai when he sent them away. Some say Hagar was already in the harem and a maidservant to Sarai in the

---

21. Genesis 16:1.

palace. Or, she could have been one of the maidservants or the daughter of one of the servants given to Abram in the initial trade. Regardless, she is with them in Canaan when Sarai loses faith that God will ever make good on his covenant. Eventually, Sarai gives Hagar to the patriarch to sleep with and conceive his child.

While this was historically a common practice, I have a hard time believing that any woman at any time in history ever enjoyed being used as a surrogate for her master's lineage. I imagine Hagar's contempt for Sarai begins here. When she conceives, Hagar's disdain for her mistress grows and Sarai mistreats her—so severely that Hagar takes off on the road through the Desert of Shur, back to Egypt. I wonder, was she so young and naive that she didn't realize what she was doing, traversing the desert while pregnant? Or, was the abuse so bad that it didn't matter, she just had to escape? What courage she must have had to choose self-protection over helpless submission.

It is on the road to Shur, while stopped at a spring, that the angel of the Lord appears to Hagar. Scholars suggest this is the preincarnate Christ. He has heard her in her misery and he asks, "Where have you come from and where are you going?"

Where have you come from, God asks Hagar. *What is your story?*

Whatever I have learned of the importance of story, I have learned from Dr. Dan Allender, creator of Story Workshops, author of *To Be Told*, and professor and founding president of the Seattle School of Theology and Psychology. He was also mentor to my husband in grad school. Hagar is not the first to whisper to my soul: *Beth, what is your story?* Dan says, "We don't just have stories; we *are* a story. It is our responsibility to know our story so we can live it out more intentionally and boldly for the Great Story, the gospel. We are to read our past to gain a greater sense of how to write our life in the present."[22] In Hagar, we are being lured to read our past. *What is your story?*

For my daughter, it is a magical place she has little memory of. At home, we retell stories and live among relics. We speak Turkish as our private parent language and host guests from our time there. I cook Turkish food and we sing "Happy Birthday" in Turkish. One would think we were immigrants. It is a part of our soul, our family culture, our story. We lived there for seven years, but it feels like an eternity.

And there is something of me still there.

Ella and I are both in need of the answer to this question: Where have you come from? Most adults eventually run into something from *before* that they need to deal with to go *beyond*. It is sometimes serious and painful. Abuse seems to be top contender. Unanswered questions spawned in every child's heart, "Do you see me?" or "Do I have what it takes?" are normal. Absent or distant mothers and fathers shape our own parenting and if there is nothing specific, our own children seem to pull all the baggage to the forefront whether we are ready or not.

My something is Turkey. What is yours?

I have sensed for quite some time now, the eight swelling years since we've returned to the States, that I left a part of me there, on the streets of Istanbul. I have been tethered. For a while, in the early days of our return, my heart needed tending to. It wasn't ready to debrief or make meaning of it all. I knew my faith took a beating, my faith

---

22. Dan Allender, *To Be Told* (Colorado Springs: Water Brook Press, 2005), 52.

in people and teammates and the Bible. My sense of calling and purpose got fuzzy. And even when I began to encounter Jesus differently, seeing Him in a new and crazy way in a graduate program in international community development, I was still skeptical of the Bible. I was wounded and raw and knowingly tread carefully upon my little soul. So did God. He waited.

But I knew we had to talk about Turkey.

In the seventh year the daily remembering began. As Ella began exuding preteen angst (Who am I?) I began living in a surreal and sensory live photo album. Daily there was a comment or person or activity that seemed to lead back to Turkey. Our stories were coming of age at the same time. God had us on a journey together. We needed to return. Unless we answered, "Where have you come from?" I sensed we would not be able to answer, "Where are you going?"

Fredrick Buechner challenges us with the revisiting of these unanswered questions, "Memory makes it possible for us both to bless the past, even those parts of it that we have always felt cursed by, and also to be blessed by it."[23] I knew I was tethered to Turkey. I sensed that my daughter and I both had heart mending and story work to do in this exotic land halfway around the world.

Fellow mom, what are you tethered to? What in your story do you need to tend to in order to move beyond? Our daughters need us to bless the past so that they can freely answer God's question, "Where are you going?" For some, childhood trauma shapes your parenting. Perhaps fear of being a distracted or absent parent has turned you into a helicopter mom. Maybe a constant childhood unease with finances has fueled your career and perfectionism,

23. Fredrick Buechner, *Telling Secrets* (San Francisco: Harper One, 2000), 33.

leading to anxiety in your family. Could infertility have altered your view of God and the amount of grace you extend to your adopted daughter? We all have a story into which our daughters have entered. Do you know yours? Will you seek to name your story so that you can root your daughter in it?

Jenni's Experience:

She has looked at the photo book I have of being pregnant and her birth for many years. Some of the sleeves are empty, because she has taken them to create a scrapbook of her life. She has asked a lot of questions about her birth and the small coastal town where she was born. There have never been any questions about her dad's absence in the photos. The longing to go there and see the place where she was born had been stirring for a couple of years.

I knew I wanted to take her there to launch her Becoming year and for her to see and hear the story of our family. Her story started with separated parents who were in the midst of a spiritually abusive community (a lot of relational confusion and chaos). After her birth, she left the hospital with a sad, lonely, and scared single mom. It was not what I had envisioned for our lives.

Her dad met her for the first time at four months old when we got back together to rebuild our marriage and family. We moved out West to start over soon afterward.

Right before her twelfth birthday she and I returned to the beach town to see the places and tell her our story. I told her about the people in the photos and explained why her dad wasn't in them. Then we made our way to the regional hospital where she took her first breath. Her dad surprised her and met us there, so that twelve years later, the three of us could leave the hospital together. God sees and He restores.

Hagar honestly answers the Lord's question, "Where have you come from?" *I have come from mistreatment. I have come from a couple who doubts you, Lord, who take matters into their own hands and treat me poorly.* And without even needing to say it, God knows. He hears her misery, knows she is with child, and sees her intimately.

You've come from mistreatment, sweet Hagar (I imagine him saying "sweet Hagar" because I picture her to be either really young or abused), *but I am asking you to return. I am asking you to go back to your mistress, but go with a promise.* And the Lord proceeds to promise Hagar the very same thing Abram is promised a chapter before: descendants too numerous to count. Sometimes God hears us in our misery but doesn't rescue us. He asks us to return with His promise: I see you. *El Roi*, the God who sees. Hagar gives God a name we see only here. An intimate seeing, not the omnipresent, omniscient seeing God, but the personal, knowing God, El Roi.

Where have you come from Hagar? *I've come from mistreatment, but I know my God sees.*

I have scrimped and saved to surprise Ella for her twelfth birthday with a journey to find our story. This is the beginning of her yearlong rites of passage. I pick her up from school to go out to lunch with suitcases in the trunk. We head straight for our plane bound for Turkey.

I walk the cobblestone streets with Ella. We are meandering up the hill toward our first Turkish apartment when we pass the Bead café—the skinny five-story aqua-blue building that holds so many of my prayers, tears, and deep wrestling with other staff and interns. The little first-floor space opens up to a garden patio, surrounded by balconies and clotheslines, but covered by grapevines. Just far enough from the cacophony of taxis and throngs of people, it was my refuge. I stand still in the entryway, remembering the cappuccinos, the cork journal, Annie, Nazan...

God saw me here.

We have tea at the café then continue up the hill. The bakery is still in business. I want to pause and weep, touch the door that was miraculously open that night so many years ago. I show Ella the place where her dad was stabbed, the counter he went behind to see the gash, the blood. I show her the taxi stand, just across the street, which provided a rushed lift to the hospital, where I waited uncomfortably for hours, already four months pregnant with her. And the mercies pour forth: the surgeon spoke English, the blade just missed the femoral artery, the assailants mugged others that night, proving it wasn't a personal attack. God saw.

The streets teem with memory: we watched the planes crash the second tower in that shop; we met with the crisis counselor after the martyrdom in that office; we had team mediation there. The stress of living cross-culturally, the loneliness of having babies and toddlers, the unmet expectations of ministry are as real as they were eight years ago. I have held on for so long.

God whispers, *I saw.*

Where have I come from? I came from stress and struggle, persecution and pain, and year after year, God asked me to return. *Go back. But go with my promise. I see you.* And in the midst of tears and memory lane I finally see what He has for me to see. All this time, I have imagined that Hagar, upon meeting the Lord at the well, returned with strength to her abusive mistress. Sure, the Lord sees, but her strength propelled her back. I can identify. All those years of stress and struggle, I never allowed for weakness. It was not an option. There was no room (in my psyche) for fatigue, fear, or futility. Yet here I was, reliving it through Ella's eyes, and weeping for that Beth. I felt all the feelings I never let her feel. I was sad. I was scared. I was weary. I felt not enough and too much and like a failure most of the time. And I have carried shame for eight years.

Where have you carried shame?

Then I see her. Hagar. She is at the well and the Lord has spoken. El Roi has seen her. And she is sad. She is scared. She feels weary. She is too much and not enough. She feels shame. But she returns. Weak, yet strong, she returns. And I hear God say, "Weakness and strength coexist and are beautiful." You were beautiful to me then. You are beautiful to me now.

As I walked streets with a child of equal height, whose little hand I used to squeeze as I pulled her from screeching taxis or disgruntled stray dogs, I am untethered. Released. I have finally answered, *Where have you come from?* I can leave the shame at the well.

Have you left your shame at the well?

My dear, sweet daughter had no memories. What little remained was concocted from days at the park with her babysitter and the nostalgic musings we've kept alive for the last eight years. Her version of Turkey was a mystical utopian community. The crowds and vast cityscape, call to prayer echoing from mosque to mosque across valleys, and sheer number of modes of transportation overwhelmed her. How could this place that is so deeply entrenched in our family story be so unfamiliar? To say she was stunned would be an understatement. And yet, it was clear her soul was also untethered.

By answering Hagar's question, *Where have you come from?*, we rooted ourselves in the Bruno narrative. Ella's place of entry into our story was my pain. In the midst of my mustered strength and courage, she entered the world. Is it any wonder that she is strong? Sensitive? Adventurous? To fully release these parts of herself without shame requires her to know her past. Otherwise, she too will wrestle with being too much or not enough. Brené Brown says, "We need to cultivate our story to let go of shame, and we need to develop our shame resilience in order to cultivate our story."[24]

Dear Mom, where have you come from? Into what story was your daughter born? Might I encourage you to join Hagar as you journey through your story and find the God who sees. Untether your soul and in so doing, release your daughter into her own story.

How you choose to launch your rites of passage year will vary with the unique women you are. Not everyone will want or be able to take a trip, but I encourage you to craft a special, out-of-the-ordinary experience that clearly marks the beginning of an intentional yearlong journey. The following chart provides some questions for you to start considering the elements of your family story and brainstorming ideas to impart this to your daughter. We have all been

---

24. Brené Brown, *The Gifts of Imperfection* (Center City, MN: Hazeldon, 2010), 40.

shaped by different places on the timeline of our lives. For some, it may be a childhood home while for others it is where they met their spouse or where that professor first spoke a dream into their soul. The places in which you still feel tethered are the places that probably hold the most power for your family narrative and thus, your daughter's future.

Hagar begins the year of *Becoming*. The foundation has been laid. It is time to construct the scaffolding of womanhood our girls need to be able to answer, *Where are you going?* and enter God's story for them.

Questions for you:

1. What is there from your past that God wants to reframe so that you can move beyond and into a new future?

2. Where have you come from? Can you name a time, like Hagar, when God asked you to return? Did you return with strength and weakness? Did you return with the confidence that God saw you?

3. If you haven't yet named the places and times in your story in which God saw, would you do so now?

4. As you consider your daughter, how can you help answer this question *Where have you come from?* What is *your* family's narrative?

5. List the people, places, or passions you want to invite your daughter into. Where and how can

you impart this to her? Perhaps the following chart will help:

Places of Importance to Our Story	What Stories Are Held There?	Who Were the Characters in These Stories?	Where Did God See Me in These Stories?	Activities to Plan to Impart This to My Daughter	Gift to Give Her so that She Remembers

Part 2

A SCAFFOLDING OF
WOMANHOOD FOR GIRLS

5

Crafting a Yearlong
Rites of Passage

Our Anthem

We had not been to a concert since 1993, when Steven Curtis Chapman's *Great Adventure* tour came to Chicago and a group of college friends bought tickets. Our unsophisticated musicality dismays our friends, Greg and Jess, who are pretty avid and regular concertgoers, particularly if the venue is Red Rocks. Do you know this place? A magnificent natural rock formation with astounding acoustics just outside of Denver. Though my in-laws used to live down the street, I had never been to an event. Jess knew the Piano Guys would get us there and this is how we found ourselves sitting outside one August night, stunned by the cellist and pianist making beauty on stage. Two instruments, countless screens showing breathtaking imagery, and heart-swelling mash-ups.

I know just enough about music to be moved by it. And I know that when the Piano Guys played their mash-up of "Fight Song" and "Amazing Grace" I lost it. I wish books could carry soundtracks. If this were possible, this is the song I would want you to hear. It is soul swelling, awe inspiring, and reaches a crescendo before dropping into a refrain of "Amazing Grace." I have no idea if this is proper music terminology. This is just how my heart feels when I hear this arrangement. I know enough of the lyrics to "Fight Song" (thanks to my three kids) to embrace it as an anthem for *Becoming*.

I envision a generation of girls who bring the fullness of themselves to the kingdom of God—a generation who finds the power of their voice and uses it to fight. We need our daughters to fight for love, for justice, for righteousness, for shalom so that God's glory is made manifest in them and in His creation. And so, fellow mothers, will you join me?

Imagine the Red Rocks Amphitheatre full of women and their daughters. Imagine the Lord's breath descending, calling us good, calling us powerful, calling us beautiful, calling us purposed. He is proud of us. He is excited to see us find our voice and offer it to His creation. And then we hear the notes to "Amazing Grace": *"Amazing grace, how sweet the sound, that saved a wretch like me. I once was lost, but now am found. Was blind but now I see."* He stretches out His arms and they cover us all and He says one word, *Grace*. My grace I give you. My grace saves you. My grace hovers near. My grace goes before and behind you. In the process of *Becoming*, remember you are designed in strength and you are covered in grace.

As you begin the process of crafting a yearlong rites of passage for your daughter, a gift indeed, my prayer for us all is this:

> God of grace and mercy, hover near. Walk alongside of us as we lead our daughters into the bigger story you are telling. Grant us the surprise of perfect timing, the delight of well-designed examples, the joy of connection and the utter beauty of what You have for us to discover.

Nuts and Bolts

The Ideal Age

While it is never too late to be intentional with your daughter, I do think the year between her twelfth and thirteenth birthday is significant and an ideal time for a rites of passage. Having said that, every girl is different and only you know yours best. But a couple of things are at work in the majority of girls' lives during this year. Culturally, becoming a teen is a well-marked birthday and a lot of hype builds the anticipation in our daughters. Physically, most girls have begun or are somewhere in the process of puberty by now and their bodies and emotions are causing confusion and anxiety. They need our focus and attention now more than ever before. This is scary stuff for most.

It should be mentioned that this is when many girls turn against their mothers. Her fear and confusion is masked by angst, anger, even hatred. Every time Mom gets near, she pulls away. I want to believe that some of this can be prevented by the attention and intention afforded in the *Becoming* year. However, for some relationships, a season of repair and trust building will precede all else. This is when moms need to be laser focused on who their daughter is, studying and researching her like a heart surgeon. Your precision will be paramount in gaining her trust and affection again. This will feel insufficient for you moms and so I've suggested some resources in the appendix for you to learn more.

Ideally, a rites of passage process at this age preempts the messages our daughters will hear and absorb from peers, school, and media. If they view mom as the purveyor of truth and the model of womanhood, I believe they will be more resilient to all else that counters our message. Let's be the first ones to engage the body, boys, and besties topics as well as cast a vision for who they are becoming as they enter their teens.

Design Your Scaffolding

I hope you feel the freedom to craft this year in a way unique to your daughter. The five categories I've chosen and wrote about are certainly not the only aspects to womanhood a girl should learn. The action words used are meant to convey a sense of immediacy and movement. As we call our daughters to join a global sisterhood and offer the fullness of who she is to God's kingdom, I believe these capture the essence of a voice becoming.

You may want to follow the same categories, but insert different films or activities (see appendix). My goal in this section is to show you what our year looked like and the meaning I derived from all that we did in order to cast a vision for who she is becoming. My goal is to inspire you!

As you reflect on the questions from part one, you may decide on different categories. Your story and your daughter's story should determine what this year looks like. If you have not spent time considering your own story and answering some of those questions, I encourage you to pause here and take some time to do that. If you're ready to go, grab the blank charts in the appendix and start brainstorming!

Make a Plan

When will you begin? I chose to launch on Ella's twelfth birthday, but we did not conclude until a few weeks after her thirteenth. Nothing magical happens on *the day*, but it was certainly fun to take her out of school and straight to the airport on her actual birthday! Look at your family and work calendar and try to make a chart of the year. Are there any special events, trips, concerts, et cetera that you know about and want to include? When I learned that Malala was coming to Denver, I switched around *Women Lead* and *Women Fight* so that hearing her speak fit in with what we were talking about. A visit to family determined which part of the year we did *Women Love* because I knew I wanted my mom and sisters to participate.

As I mentioned in chapter two, I made a sketch of the year with my ideas of books, films, and activities, but allowed God to surprise us with the unexpected. It became a working plan. When November and December filled up with holidays and travel, we completely paused and did nothing around *Becoming.* There were times we jam-packed a weekend with experiences and weeks when nothing special happened except book conversations. My point is this: while it is yearlong, it does not have to be intense and time consuming. It requires a plan and demands your attention, but relax and have fun with it!

After you have a sketch of the year, make a budget. What will this cost you? Maybe jot down expenses next to your ideas. Books (borrow or buy?), films (rent versus attend?), events, and trips all add up. See the appendix for ideas of how to fund *Becoming.* I want to encourage you to pray over your plan and ask God to help you creatively afford it. In the absence of disposable income, my husband and I made sacrifices, sold things, and thought outside of the box. You can too.

Clearly Begin and Clearly End

Ancient rites of passage traditions always had a clear beginning and end. Youth knew without question when they were declared a woman, a man. When they emerged from the tent, the forest, the night by themselves, they were celebrated, blessed, and welcomed into the company of adults. Though intentional parenting has no beginning or end, defining the parameters of the year of *Becoming* is crucial. Girls need to understand that they are embarking on a meaningful, well-constructed, purposeful year that will culminate in some sort of test and invitation to join a sisterhood of women. She does not necessarily need to know the details, but you may want to give her a sketch of the categories she will learn about and a hint of a "test" at the end. I think it's important our daughters understand the weight of what we're bestowing upon them: a voice becoming.

In our family, our kids expect their year to begin at age twelve and that sometime close to their thirteenth birthday, the legacy event occurs. My husband's years of research and counseling men confirmed the need for boys to prove themselves and be named a man by other men. For his test, our son went on a five-mile hike alone, encountering men with scenario challenges along the way. Each time he correctly answered the scenario, he received a brick. By the time he reached his destination, he was carrying six bricks (the weight of being a man). Three other men joined my husband who blessed and gifted him, signifying he passed. (The gift was a Gandalf staff!) Our girls watched and waited. They also need to prove they have what it takes. While each of their tests will look different, they will each be about showing their grit, their knowledge, and their preparedness to leave childhood behind. They will each culminate in a celebration, blessing, and gift that declares the passage complete: "Welcome to womanhood."

Tamara's Story

Inspired by the Maya Angelou poem, "The year of Phenomenal Women" was the name of Kayla's Becoming year. Guided by the Fruits of the Spirit,

*each of our outings began with the gift of a stained
glass from a local Kenyan artist and included a relevant Bible study and some combination of an event,
book, movie, or song.*

*We started with a lavish night at the Kenyan
hotel where President Obama stayed as we explored
what love means from 1 Corinthians 13. After learning how to make sushi and feasting on our creations,
we snuggled up to watch movies and I tucked her in
by reading our worn copy of* I Love You as Much *and singing "Some Say Love," a song I often sang
to the kids at bedtime.*

*Other outings were more simple—we went out
for lunch to discuss patience as we studied Psalm
40 and reread "Wangari's Trees of Peace," the story
of Wangari Maathai, a phenomenal Kenyan woman
whose patience and persistence revived Kenya's trees
through the Greenbelt Movement. She received the
Nobel Peace Prize in 2004, the same year we adopted
Kayla and her twin brother while living in Kenya.
On the way home, we listened to U2's 40 inspired
by the Psalm and talked about our upcoming camping trip to Aberdare National Park where our family
would see the beauty of Wangari's trees. Of course,
the stained glass for patience was a tree!*

*We concluded the year with another night at a
hotel where we completed a 5K and saw the female
frontrunners at mile sixteen of a local marathon. The
last stained glass was a rainbow finish line represent-
ing self-control that I gave to Kayla as we left for
church where she and her brother were baptized by
their father later that morning.*

*These nine stained glasses now hang across
Kayla's window as a reminder of what it means to*

become a phenomenal woman and grow in love,
joy, peace, patience, kindness, goodness, faithfulness,
gentleness, and self-control.

Underlying Key Elements

In chapter two, I explained the ethos of a *Becoming* year: a
paradigm of being. I wrote about the role of you and your
story, the role of other women, and the role of dad and
how they are key characters in a good rites of passage for
girls. Now I'd like you to consider the role of key elements
interwoven into the year's design. As you read the following
chapters, you'll see how these are inherent in my discussions
and activities with my daughter.

The Power of Interpretation

When I was a full eight months pregnant, we flew from
Turkey to Virginia seeking answers for our next step in ministry. We left two kids with grandparents and drove up to
northern Virginia to hear this guy speak. He would change
our entire future. I do not remember much. I remember
some funny stories. Oh, how I love his stories! I remember
thinking he was making up words because surely you can't
make nouns out of verbs like that. I remember concluding,
yes, we will move to Seattle and study with this man. But
that's about it. What I did not expect was *her*: Ronna, the
colleague who joined Dr. Dan Allender for one portion of
the conference.[25]

---

25. Mars Hill Graduate School Conference, April 2006, Falls River
Church, Virginia.

The notes I took from Ronna's talk have been tucked in Bibles and planners for the past ten years, always at the ready. The way she talked about a story I had heard countless times rocked my entire perception of the Bible. If I had so missed this one, what others was I missing? Where do you get these glasses to read with such a varied lens? In fact, if is there is a birthplace to my story of empowering women, it may have been that day with Ronna.

The story: the woman at the well. The scandalous, sinful woman in her sixth relationship...or was she? In a culture in which men divorced women and women were stoned for uncleanliness, how is this woman still alive after five divorces? Furthermore, how could she have persevered through so much (be it divorce or death) and still be pursued by men? Was she that provocative? Intriguing? She is certainly intelligent, capable of a theological discussion with Jesus. She must have been privy to more religious education than most women. And here she is with the Messiah. A woman carrying shame and self-contempt receives none from this man. He engages her. Finds her intriguing. Pursues her. She leaves the well an empowered woman with a voice. She returns to the place in which she has only ever known shame and speaks boldly, with confidence, becoming the first evangelist in the New Testament.

I am sitting there, considering the Samaritan woman in a whole new light when Ronna says, "The primary work of the interpreter (exegete) is not to read what is there, but what is not there." Ten years ago, as I jotted this down, I had no idea how real the words would become. I had no idea I would infuse my parenting with this definition. I did not realize that she was speaking the words of *Becoming*. The role of moms with our daughters is to read what is not there and speak into the chasm. Our role is to name the invisible so our girls have eyes to see a different story. We are exegetes, interpreters of the invisible narrative unfolding in their lives. Do you have eyes to see and to name?

In Genesis 1 God begins to name and sort. In chapter two, He grants that honor to Adam. A new narrative has begun. We name with the tools and words we have at the time, but sometimes, we get it wrong. Sometimes, we have to go back and renarrate. We have to look with a different lens, weathered by time and experience, and see if there is truth to the naming we've done.[26] So it's okay to be a little timid of being an exegete in your daughter's life. I think the key is curiosity.

If we're curious interpreters, we approach the scaffolding with our daughters like this example: "Women lead when they use their gifts, talents, and skills to influence others for the greater good. I've noticed when you get a creative and exciting new idea your friends pay attention. You're really good at rallying people. I wonder how you could let God use that in you for the greater good instead of using it to have more power over friends?" If we're good at exegesis, we've just named something maybe even our daughters have not yet seen about themselves. Maybe our curiosity alters their story a bit.

The Value of Experience

In *The Underground Girls of Kabul*, investigative reporter Jenny Nordberg tells the story of Azita, a female parliamentarian who unsuccessfully runs for a second term. During the election, she is on national television and views the publicity

---

26. Sandra Hopkins, Reclaiming Remnants Workshop, November 2015, Wellington, Colorado.

as a win in and of itself—girls must see women in these roles to imagine another future.[27] Girls must see and experience the scaffolding we build so they can imagine how they fit into it. "We care for only what we love. We love only what we know. We truly know only what we experience."[28]

A few years ago, when two of our three kids were studying U.S. history, we were able to take them to Colonial Williamsburg. Having grown up in Virginia, I fondly remembered the historic town and live demonstrations of the tradesmen. But a lot has changed and now street theater brings to life this living museum. We walked among costumed townspeople, watched an agitated argument break out in front of the governor's mansion between patriots and rebels, and heard the first reading of the recently delivered Declaration of Independence in front of the courthouse. I wish actors had been at Independence Hall in Philadelphia when we visited because the tour guide did not do it justice! You can imagine, experiencing history versus reading about it are two entirely different things.

We truly know what we experience. Moms, let's give our daughters experiences that help them know themselves, know the world, and know God's heart. Let's give them opportunities to wrestle with life and mature through the process. This is why a yearlong passage is invaluable. They need time to thoroughly absorb and digest experiences around each scaffolding category.

---

27. Jenny Nordberg, *Underground Girls of Kabul: In Search of Resistance in Afghanistan* (New York: Crown, 2014), 58.

28. Steven-Bouma Prediger, *For the Beauty of the Earth: A Christian Vision for Creation Care*, 2nd ed. (Grand Rapids, MI: Baker Academic, 2010), 21, as quoted in Ken Wytsma's *Pursuing Justice*, 275.

The Role of Metaphor

We are a storied people. We relish stories. We are stories. And through stories we learn.

This begins when children are little and we read about the tortoise and the hare or the boy who cried wolf. To these tales we ascribe meaning. Jesus did the same thing through parables, which comprise nearly one-third of his teachings. Part of the beauty of *Becoming* is learning through story: yours, hers, and other women. This is why carefully curating books, films, and even songs are an integral part of the year. Your daughter will be learning through a variety of senses, all based upon story.

Looking at life as metaphor helps us name that which is too often invisible. It brings story into everyday living. It shifts our perspective as we see through a different lens. It distills the abstract into concrete tangible lessons. And it is such a valuable tool for parenting![29] Metaphor framed the night I re-created an ancient red tent ceremony for my daughter. As women, the fundamental thing we share is our monthly cycle. As family, our bloodline connects us in a different way. But as sisters, we share stories of love. In a red-cast room, we feasted on sweets, stories, and marked blood lines on our body with henna. We ascribed meaning to love through metaphor.

The last writing retreat I took to finish this book was at an abbey in the Rocky Mountains. One afternoon, after convincing myself that a mountain lion was stalking me in the boulders, I searched for an open path and discovered the stations of the cross. Fifteen large wooden crosses lined

---

29. "Biking as a Metaphor for Life and Other Things I Tell Myself While Trying to Survive the Netherlands on Two Wheels," May 25, 2016, https://www.bethbruno.org/blog/biking-as-a-metaphor-for-life-and-other-things-i-tell-myself-while-trying-to-survive-the-netherlands-on-two-wheels.

the path and a small metal engraving of the scenes of the crucifixion hung in the middle. It struck me, as I walked between numbers two and nine and the cross seemed to get heavier and heavier upon Christ, that the cross is truly the ultimate metaphor. Jesus bore the sins of the world upon his back and the weight nearly buried him. In the seventh scene, Jesus sinks to his knees under the burden of our sin, and appropriately this was the cross with the most rocks perched upon the crossbeam. I'm not sure what Catholics mean by this, but it felt symbolic to heap our sin (rocks) upon this cross of all the crosses. As the ultimate parent, God knew how powerful metaphors are for story-based teaching.

A Blessing

My prayer for you and your daughter is that you would know, in the core of your being, God knit you together in his strength and in his grace. He fashioned in you a purpose, "to join him in the work he does, the good work he has gotten ready for us to do, work we had better be doing."[30] Dear sisters, let's call our daughters to that. Let's lift their eyes above the cacophony of teendom and inspire them to live for a bigger story. God's story is so remarkably, stunningly, absolutely worth it.

> Oh Lord, send forth these mother-daughter pairs to reflect you and your kingdom. Bless every small inten-
> tional step this mom takes to usher her daughter into discovering her voice. God, journey with them in this process of *Becoming*. Hem them in with your grace. Amen.

---

30. Ephesians 2:10 (MSG).

My *Becoming* Working Plan

Becoming Category	Working Definition	Time Frame	Who Else?
Launch: "Where have you come from?"	To live intentionally into God's story, it is essential our daughters know their family story.	12th birthday April 29	Friends in Turkey
Women Lead	Women lead by wrestling with an unknown future on behalf of another.	May–June	Dad
Women Love	When women love fiercely, with other women, an intense beauty and capacity for good is unleashed.	July–August	Aunts, Grandma
Women Fight	Women fight as warriors fueled by the passions of redemption.	September–October	Jenni, Jess
Women Sacrifice	Women sacrifice as they humble themselves to others without losing their voice.	January–February	Brother, Sister
Women Create	Women create life and beauty through our actions, words, and choices.	March–April	Sandy, AJ, Dad
Legacy Event: "Where are you going?"	While they will not know the answer to this question at age 13, it is imperative our daughters know it is a question to ask: Where are you going as you discover your role in God's story?	May	Grandma

6

Women Lead

Anyone who wrestles with an uncertain future on behalf of others—anyone who uses her gifts, talents, and skills to influence the direction of others for the greater good—is a leader.[31]

—Dan Allender

I love the story my mom tells of my first dance recital. Of course, as memories go, it is augmented by the photos: pre-Instagram squares of naturally occurring haze. I am onstage for the tap show in a fringed pink satin leotard with about twenty other preschoolers. Because of my height, I am in the middle with little heads cascading down to my left and right. You can imagine. It is chaos. No one turns the right way or spins on cue, and half of the little girls are looking for a parent's face. My grandfather is laughing so hard he is crying. This is vivid in my mind. I'm not sure if I saw the video once and could hear his laughter or if this is just the portion of the story I treasure most. But at some point in the routine, I take charge. I start pulling arms to get the others in line

31. Dan Allender, *Leading with a Limp: Turning Your Struggles into Strengths* (Colorado Springs: Water Brook Press, 2006), 25.

and bossing around my classmates onstage. Firstborn all the way, I'm determined to bring order to this mess.

Striving and clamoring to lead has been my story ever since.

Growing up, being a good kid and a good student lent itself to class office and team captain, but did that mean I could inspire people? Teachers frequently told me I was a good leader, but I sensed they really meant role model. After all, I was not the girl with the entourage in tow through the hallways of our school. Sure, I was often full of ideas (I started a sticker club and a friend newsletter—the eighties version of Facebook), but did innovation mean I was a leader? In college, I enrolled in the Undergraduate Leadership Program to verify if I was indeed endowed with this gift. As a part of a campus ministry group, leadership felt like *the* spiritual gift to have, and I was developing an unhealthy envy to possess it.

My story weaves through the muddied waters of American women of faith in my generation, navigating motherhood and ambition, constantly wondering if I was spending my time wisely, always wanting more of what I wasn't currently doing. I was in ministry for most of my kids' little years, which offered flexibility but often sidelined me without asking. It seemed that I always wanted more responsibility or thought I could handle more when it wasn't being offered or asked of me. I had the burden and privilege of having influence without position or title, of working without receiving a paycheck with my name on it. We were a ministry family. I was *his* wife, *their* mom. They were my top priority and greatest herd to shepherd (the ministry term for *leadership*). If I was too ambitious, I felt like too much in the eyes of teammates. If I failed to fit the mold, I felt like not enough. My too much-ness and not enough-ness were exhausting.

To be honest, in certain seasons, this was more disheartening than I could handle. I started to have an image of myself that went like this: I was sitting in an auditorium surrounded by people. To my left and right were friends and coworkers, changing on the season. From stage, an honor was announced. It doesn't matter what the honor was—a position, an award, some sort of recognition. The spotlight scanned the room, and as it landed on the person next to me, their name was proclaimed loudly. Repeatedly I felt like the runner-up, the sidekick, the supportive friend or teammate, but never the Leader.

I cannot ignore my story as I raise my daughter to understand how women lead. I see too many women reliving their adolescence through their children, striving for the recognition they sought at that age or pushing girls to do more than they achieved themselves. Furthermore, many of us who strive for so long to find our voice end up having a chip on our shoulder. We must resist the temptation to direct any newfound strength and agency toward bitterness. Sarah Bessey reflects on the power of women so beautifully: "As a Jesus feminist, I believe we are part of the trajectory of the redemption story for women in our churches, in our homes, in our marriages, in our parenting, in our friendships, and in our public lives. This trajectory impacts the story of humanity."[32]

Jesus loves women. And He uses women to impact the story of humanity. Beyond roles and responsibilities, I believe there is something inherent in all of us to lead for the greater good. Our daughters may grow up to be FBI analysts (my

---

32. Sarah Bessey, *Jesus Feminist: An Invitation to Revisit the Bible's View of Women* (New York: Howard Books, 2013), 30.

redo dream job), homemakers, engineers, or bookkeepers; and amid their role, I believe they are designed to lead.

We were breathless by the time we entered the Liberty Bell Center. Torrential rains had followed us throughout our spring break trip from New York to Philadelphia, and we had just sprinted from Independence Hall in time to hear a park ranger talk about the women involved in the freedom fight. I felt a kinship with Lucretia Mott and Angelina Grimké. Their perseverance and courage paved the way for the rights and privileges I enjoy today. Faithful Quakers and suffragists, they soon learned that their movement was intricately tied to the antislavery crusade and joined the ranks of Fredrick Douglass, William Lloyd Garrison, Susan B. Anthony, and Sojourner Truth. Heroes and heroines all, leading in a time of such division that the entire nation splintered. The wetness I wiped away was a mix of rain and tears. These were my sisters!

I wanted Ella to feel the courage and determination coursing through their legacy, living on in me. How do you help a modern-day teen appreciate that all she enjoys as an American girl rests on the relentless pursuit of justice by suffragists and abolitionists, civil rights activists and feminists? Girl power is a thing only because of their prework. The unquestioned opportunities for career and a life of her choosing exist only because of these sisters. And they do not exist everywhere.

Even the idea that women lead, though historic and biblical, is a privileged and nuanced principle if looked at globally. We must look beneath the surface to find examples of female business owners or teachers dedicated to reducing illiteracy and poverty among their people. At first glance, we only see patriarchal societies where girls' dreams are soon swallowed by survival. Unable to go to school because of prejudice, war, lack of sanitary pads, uniform fees, and other things we don't typically relate to school today, they resign themselves to a life of tradition, early marriage, and mother-hood. If you aren't presented with an alternative story, it's exceptional to imagine one.

I've been curating exceptional stories. And I want Ella to hear them. If she can visualize current situations for girls that illustrate the utter lack of all the privileges she enjoys, perhaps she will come to appreciate the legacy from which she has come—bold and courageous women who led out of strength and vulnerability.

It's an early summer morning when she and I eat breakfast on the floor in front of *Half the Sky*, a PBS documentary based on the book by the same name by Nicholas Kristof and Sheryl WuDunn. I have read this book twice and already watched the entire series. It is full of stories of women whom I long to meet, want to embrace, and want to throw a party for. How grand to all be in the same room, celebrating their willingness to overcome severe barriers to bring goodness and justice to their sphere of influence. Some of the stories are too brutal to expose Ella to yet, but there are some she needs to see.

Kristof travels to various locations with different Ameri-can actresses, capitalizing on their platform to help raise awareness. Were it not for their casual trekking gear and Kristof's DSLR camera, one might think we were watching a historical film. Ella surely would have thought so. Only the stark juxtaposition of Gabriella Union's fedora to the demure Vietnamese teacher gave context to the time period. These stories are current.

We watch the episodes about education and microfinance, and she learns about the lengths to which girls will travel to school in Vietnam (seventeen miles each way on a bike and a ferry) or to which mothers work to provide school fees for their children. In Kenya, we meet a mother who will go without food for a few days to save the remaining fees for her children to start school. We learn that the Kenyan men are the ones who buy the sodas in the market, but the women buy the milk and yogurt for their children. They are the ones who hide their hard-earned money, join savings clubs, and start small businesses all in hopes of elevating their children, through education, to a better life with more opportunities. All the opportunities girls like Ella take for granted.

The women and girls struggle. They sacrifice, sometimes their own food, sometimes their safety, for the sake of others. What is this in their character? What am I so drawn to, these inexplicable women of the world, that I curate their stories and soak in their triumphs? More importantly, what am I hoping to teach my daughter through their example?

These women have hope for a better future for sure, an imagination for something different than the story they are living. This is certainly a truth I want to cultivate in Ella's heart and one my husband and I have lived by. He holds out hope for his counseling clients every day as he imagines with those on the couch and gently prods them to love their story and live restored. I hold out hope for young men and women in my city, that they will not be exploited into human trafficking because of an educated, empowered community I have helped equip. Yes, hope is a key ingredient to bringing God's kingdom to earth as it is in heaven. Hope is the most powerful weapon of a leader.

But without embracing their current reality, can hope be imagined? There is something to these courageous women, to the Angelina Grimkés and Susan B. Anthonys, who face the slavery, the sexism, the lack of education, the alcoholic depressed men of the Kenyan slums, and yet are empowered to rise and embrace hope for change. Only when my husband's clients face their own story can they begin to write a new one. Even in my own processing of Turkey, I have seen that there are times when you must deal with the "before" to move "beyond." Both embracing their own story and hoping for a better future, echo the questions God asked Hagar: *Where have you come from and where are you going?* They are questions Ella and I will revisit throughout this year of *Becoming*.

In the midst of this, we are privileged to hear Malala speak. Ella has read the book *I Am Malala* and we have discussed the young Pakistani girl's bravery and commitment to girls' education. As the youngest Nobel Peace Prize recipient in history and an incredible activist, she is potentially our daughters' generation's greatest role model. When Malala first began to speak out in Pakistan, the BBC asked her to blog under a pseudonym, which turned into a radio show. Here is a girl so dedicated to and publicly outspoken about the right for girls' education in the Taliban-ruled Swat Valley that she was shot in the head to be silenced.

On the way to hear her speak, we discuss a definition of leadership I have written out on a card: "Anyone who wrestles with an uncertain future on behalf of others—anyone who uses her gifts, talents, and skills to influence the direction of others for the greater good—is a leader." We talk easily about examples of those using their gifts on behalf of others: author and speaker Jennie Allen used her influence to start IF:Gathering, an incredible ministry to women that has impacted hundreds of thousands; some of Silicon Valley's youngest tech creators have become the world's greatest philanthropists, using their billions to create foundations; and even dear old Mom and Dad are using their gifts and skills on behalf of those in our community. Authors, engineers, counselors, and community organizers can all lead *if they use their gifts to influence the direction of others for the greater good.*

Could Ella imagine her own gifts, talents, and skills? Did she have a category for how those might be used on behalf of others? She sings. She's an athlete. She's fiercely competitive. She's good in front of people and not afraid of giving speeches. She's good with little kids and the developmentally disabled. What might all that turn into if she has a heart set toward others rather than her own gain and fame?

I am crying in the first five minutes of the evening as they show the trailer for the documentary *He Named Me Malala.* Tears are streaming because Malala is just a normal girl, with normal siblings, bursting with a passion and this sense of justice and allowed to use her voice because her father is her biggest cheerleader. Later she tells the audience, "If I were a normal Pakistani girl, I would be married with children. People always ask my father what did he do and he says, 'Don't ask me what I did, ask me what I didn't do: I didn't clip her wings.'"

Who would we all be if our wings were never clipped by parents, finances, society, or limited opportunities? Who did God create us to be in all our glory?

Malala shares that she has just come from Washington, D.C., and though she met with President Obama, presented at the UN and spent the day on Capitol Hill with various congressmen and -women, the highlight of her time was Senator John Lewis. In him, the man who crossed the Selma, Alabama, bridge alongside Martin Luther King, Jr., she found a kindred spirit. Like her, he wrestled with an uncertain future on behalf of others. And like him, she hopes to live to see the change. She dreams of a day when she can tell her grandchildren about a time in history when all girls were not given an education nor treated equally.

What uncertain future will Ella wrestle on behalf of others? How about your daughter?

Personally, I wonder if all my years of clamoring after leadership roles and titles faltered because I wasn't wrestling with an unknown future on behalf of others. Sure, I could convince myself that I wanted young Turkish students to know Jesus or our young interns to mature and develop as disciples, but I know that I also wanted to feel like others thought of me as a leader; and occasionally, it would have been nice to get the plaque, the gift, the accolades too.

Now I find myself leading police officers and school principals and other amazing community stakeholders, not because I ever imagined myself doing this, but because I feel absolutely compelled to wrestle with an uncertain future on behalf of at-risk youth in our community who could be trafficked tomorrow. I will speak and write and organize and train and persist because I know that my gifts, talents, and skills can influence the direction of others for the greater good. It feels obvious to me. There is no clamoring. There just is. Something in me feels created to do this work. God's glory in me?

I think God's glory is seen in Malala too. I think her promotion of education as a means of eradicating most of the world's evil is well in line with God's heart. I think He thinks she's pretty amazing. And I think He thinks Ella is pretty amazing too. And your daughter. How has she been created to reflect His glory? Part of our job is to help them figure it out.

We watch *Cinderella*. Not the Disney animated version or one of the many remakes of the same, but the remade *Downton Abbey* actresses' version. Of course, I am struck by the repetitive mantra "Have courage and be kind," but it is one line toward the end that has me sitting up straight. I had wondered what God might have for us as we watched this movie during this phase of *Becoming*. And here it is, tucked into some of the last lines of the film, when Cinderella becomes a true heroine and truly, a remarkable leader.

The stepmother has found the glass slipper and locked Cinderella in the attic. But the prince has issued a decree promising to marry the girl who shows up at the castle with the slipper. Concocting a villainous plot with the grand duke, the stepmother comes to the attic to tell Cinderella she will be able to marry the prince only if she makes her stepmother the mistress of the household, basically granting her control of the kingdom. In a beautiful act of leadership, Cinderella says, "I could not spare my father from you, but I will spare the prince and the kingdom from you." Trading her life for the good of the prince and kingdom sounds eerily familiar.

In Mark 10:44–45 we're told, "Whoever wants to be first among you, must be a slave. Even the son of man did not come to be served, but to serve and to give his life as a ransom for many." This is the passage I have heard growing up in parachurch ministries as the premier example of servant leadership: the act of using your influence to lead for the sake of others, not to advance your own power. It is the practice of giving your life as a ransom for many.

It is what I see when I read about Sakena Yacoobi, founder of the Afghan Institute of Learning, who has endured death threats to bring education to women in Afghanistan, or when I hear about my friend serving in a patriarchal culture. She was one female among a group of males on the leadership team of a parachurch organization. When she noticed certain discrepancies and sensed something was not right with a particular leader, she risked relational harmony to do the right thing and report it to regional leadership. She and her family suffered severed relationships in their church family and team as well as emotional distress to make the ethical choice.

These are the kinds of female leaders I want to show my daughter. Not women who are power hungry or have a need to prove something. Not girl power for the sake of girl power. Not this chip on their shoulder to show the world that they are as capable as their brothers. No, it is a beautiful, humble desire to use their influence to benefit others. This is the kind of leader I desire for Ella to become and that which is most captivating about the legacy of our sisters, past and present.

Phoebe's Story

I have been searching for female leaders in Scripture and have found many. In fact, Rachel Held Evans says, "It's astounding that, in the midst of such a patriarchal culture, so many women are honored as leaders and teachers in scripture. This speaks volumes about the remarkable wisdom, resourcefulness, courage, and godliness it would take to teach and lead in such times, and says a lot about the value God places on women even when the world does not."[33]

Phoebe is one such leader.[34] We know little of her, but that she is called sister, servant, and saint by Paul. The Greek word used for *servant, diaknonos*, is also translated "deacon" in Paul's letters. In Romans 13:4 it is used as a "minister of God to you for good." It would appear Phoebe was a leader in the church, *a minister of God to you for good.* And it is believed that she is the one entrusted to carry Paul's letter to the Romans in Rome.

33. Rachel Held Evans, "Who's Who Among Biblical Women Leaders," June 6, 2012, http://rachelheldevans.com/blog/mutuality-women-leaders.
34. Romans 16.

She must have been a courageous woman, to set out on such a journey alone, and a woman of means to afford such a trip or have the business to justify it. In fact, women like Phoebe funded the gospel. Paul calls her a benefactor to himself and many others, implying she was a woman of wealth who gave generously to the work of the gospel or, according to *The Message*, a "key representative of the church of Cenchrea."[35] Regardless, as a deacon, she is one "worthy of respect, sincere, not indulging in much wine, and not pursuing dishonest gain." The job description maintained "They must keep hold of the deep truths of the faith with a clear conscience. They must first be tested; and then if there is nothing against them, let them serve as deacons."[36]

Phoebe was a leader—one who used her influence to benefit the good of others. Without her, where would the gospel be? As Malala uses her voice, and Cinderella used her silence, might our girls use something they possess to benefit others?

Ella's Experience

Just as the last of the snow melted in the Rocky Mountains, Ella and her dad went camping. They share a love of the outdoors and an equal amount of sadness that we don't live in the mountains. This was a trip designed to spend intentional time with Ella around the category of *Women Lead*. The challenge I posed: Use her skills to benefit another. What would it look like to camp with an expert yet seek to benefit him through her leadership? Though she is usually eager to help set up the tent and start the fire, this time Dad yielded entirely to her. He created space for her to use her skills (they were plenty warm by her fire) and suffered quietly in their

---

35. Romans 16:1 (MSG).
36. 1 Timothy 3:8–10 (NIV).

absence (breakfast was a little black!). Prior to the weekend, she researched hiking trails, chose the campsite and found a five-mile hike through Aspen groves.

It was less than ideal in many ways. They camped near sand dunes the first night without knowing other campers go there to drive their four-wheelers late into the darkness. On little sleep, they struck camp and started over the next day. Having borrowed a four-wheeler as well, Ella was super-excited to have a spin on the sand, only to have it die while she was driving and towed out of the valley. There were hiccups that needed to be processed. She was stretched to lead through serving when her skills were deficient or when her plans needed adjustment. But it was the hands-on experience necessary to bring full meaning to these two months of focusing on *Women Lead*. Dad gave her a long coveted pocketknife to symbolize "wrestling with an uncertain future on behalf of others."

When I think of a woman who wrestles like this, I picture Mary. Of course, the Mary I am picturing is actually closer to Ella's age than mine. She is a young girl, mature beyond her years. A quiet and faithful soul who humbly accepts her part in God's story. For whatever she imagines her role to be, surely she is uncertain yet resolved: she knows she carries the Savior, the promised one for all her people. They've been waiting. God has been silent for four hundred years and now He speaks? Now He comes to her, of all people? I consider her actions despite the circumstances: she spends the first three months of her holy pregnancy with her cousin Elizabeth, only to return home visibly and shamefully with child. Miraculously still betrothed to Joseph, they make the trek to Bethlehem late in her pregnancy, for when they show up there is no room left and she's about to give birth. Not only does she give birth in a humiliating state, but she entertains guests within days. All this because she knows in her heart, where she is treasuring all things, that her narrative is to wrestle with an unknown future on behalf of her people.

Mary is a beautiful picture of a leader who uses her gifts (the ones the Lord deemed her worthy to bear His son) to influence the direction of others for the greater good. Yet, I've never seen Mary used as an example in female leadership studies. Facing difficult circumstances, without desire to advance her own platform, she lays down her life for the story God is telling through her. Long into our daughters' future, let us pray that they lead like Mary. Like my friend on the patriarchal team and Sakeena and Malala. Let us pray that they learn to wrestle with an unknown future on behalf of others.

Moms, what story is God telling through you? As you consider your own leadership journey, how are you using your influence to benefit others? You may not call it leadership, but I would venture to guess you are doing just that whether you've named it or not. Reflecting on your own story informs how you craft this section for your daughter. The following questions and chart are guides to lead you in your own preparation. As God has designed each of us so uniquely, I imagine almost every rites of passage will look different. Who are you? Who is your daughter? What are the relevant films, books, and cultural heroes of the day? As you pray, ask for God to provide meaningful opportunities. Take advantage of where you live, who you know, and what your daughter might be up for trying! Do a little research and leave some room for God to surprise you.

Lord of ransoms and life-laying, God of leaders and
servants, may this mama and her daughter learn
what it is to use their gifts to benefit others that
You may be glorified.

Questions for you:

1. What is your story of leadership? Did you grow up struggling to know if you were a leader or not?

2. How does your story influence the way you parent your daughter?

3. How do you use your influence to benefit others? What gifts, talents, or skills do you use to influence the direction of the greater good?

4. What are aspects of leadership that you want to impart to your daughter?

5. How have you seen your daughter use her influence to benefit others? How might you orchestrate opportunities for her to rise to the challenge?

Books for Her to Read	Books I'm Reading	Scripture	Films to Watch	Activities	Gift
I Am Malala by Malala Yousafzai	*Leading with a Limp* by Dan Allender	Romans 16 (Phoebe)	*Cinderella*	Go hear Malala speak	A pocketknife
	Half the Sky by Nicholas Kristof and Sheryl WuDunn	Mark 10:44–45	*Half the Sky*	Plan and lead a camping trip with Dad	
	The Invention of Wings by Sue Monk Kidd				

Books for Her to Read	Books I'm Reading	Scripture	Films to Watch	Activities	Gift

7

Women Love

Let us be women who Love, in spite of fear.
Let us be women who Love, in spite of our stories.
Let us be women who Love loudly, beautifully, Divinely.
Let us be women who Love.
— Idelette McVicker[37]

I have a disclaimer to make. I am a really well-loved woman. And I know that just now some of you might want to write me off, close the book. Because you are suffering. You've suffered. And I can't possibly get it. You're tempted to skip this chapter because it's going to sound hollow and happy-clappy. I have two loving, still-married parents and a husband of twenty-plus years who is seriously my best friend. And it struck me the other day, saying goodbye to a recently divorced friend, that so much of my inner core comes from this stable, authentic love. It's real and I need to acknowledge it. I am loved.

37. Idelette McVicker, "Manifesto: Let Us Be Women Who Love," http://shelovesmagazine.com/manifesto/.

At the same time, I realize I am loved with a far greater love than earthly relationships. And this is real too. I met him when I was fourteen.

My purity-loving friends had invited me to a youth group ski trip. Having already experienced being pushed down the slope in the wedge position at our nearby ski resort, I thought I could surely handle the moguls my group was tackling at this larger ski area. I remember facing Cupp Run with a pit in my stomach and snow plowing left to right, pausing atop each mogul before carefully turning to crisscross the mountain. It took me two and a half hours to descend and one lone friend stuck with me, Alex. That night in the lodge, I was wiped. But the speaker grabbed my attention. Randy Matthews had crazy red hair and a pre–*Duck Dynasty* era beard. He wore snakeskin boots and talked about Jesus like he knew him. He described a personal relationship with a loving father whom I thought I knew, but seriously began to question as Randy continued. I spent the night grilling Randy Matthews in the hallway, eager to know this God-man, eager to understand this love that Jesus offered me.

But I took it. I took it and lodged it in my soul and it's been growing ever since and the crazy thing...the crazy thing about God's love is that it turns us into lovers.[38] "We love because he first loved us."[39] The ultimate source of strength, beauty, compassion, and love is God's love. He is the reason we Christians have a fighting chance of standing apart from the world. As Sarah Bessey describes, women who are loved and free are beautiful. And a free woman? "She is loved. She is rising. She is awake at last, and as the Chinese proverb says, when sleeping women wake, mountains

38. Eddy Hopkins, sermon, August 23, 2015.
39. 1 John 4:19 (NIV).

move. She is secure in the love and freedom of her God; she knows the voice of Jesus down in her bones and therefore, she loves."[40]

Women who know they are loved rise up, secure in that love, and move mountains.

I went to college to make money. I left the rolling hills of Virginia for the skyscrapers of Chicago with a dream of making commercials that made me lots of money. I wanted to work on Michigan Avenue and wear cute business suits to work. And I was a young Christian.

I hadn't fully thought my plan through because my college actually didn't even have a marketing department. I switched to Communication Studies and learned that the head of the department was starting a leadership program. Remember my leadership questions? I enrolled and off we went into the city to visit, not CEOs in skyscrapers, but founders and directors of nonprofits seeking to bring social change to Chicago. We were far from Michigan Avenue when God began to nudge his way into my greedy heart's plans. When my suitemate asked me to read a book she was reading, *There Are No Children Here* by Alex Kotlowitz, I had no idea I was about to experience my first "brain ninja" (this is a sly move God does from out of nowhere to turn your world upside down).

Kotlowitz spent a year with a family in the projects of Chicago, documenting their living conditions, school environment, and neighborhood violence. I was left without words. Except God had them for me. The night I finished the book, I sat in my dorm bunk bed and composed a letter I titled "A Call to Prayer." I had no idea I would soon live in a land that

---

40. Sarah Bessey, *Jesus Feminist: An Invitation to Revisit the Bible's View of Women* (New York: Howard Books, 2013), 135.

actually called forth such a prayer across the city five times a day. I implored its recipients to pray for the poor children of Chicago. I mailed it to every friend, family friend, and relative I knew. The book wrecked my world. I changed my major. Changed my summer plans. And woke up.

I had responded to the voice of Jesus in my bones. I knew it was Him. It was Him breaking my heart for the kids that were breaking His. Loving Jesus ransacked me because it made me vulnerable to His voice. It was only a matter of time before He would talk to me about making lots of money through advertising to entice people to buy things they didn't know they needed. He was calling me to love more deeply—to love Him and others and even myself with a far greater love.

C. S. Lewis challenges us: "There is no safe investment. To love at all is to be vulnerable. Love anything, and your heart will be wrung and possibly broken. If you want to make sure of keeping it intact, you must give it to no one, not even an animal. Wrap it carefully round with hobbies and little luxuries; avoid all entanglements; lock it up safe in the casket or coffin of your selfishness. But in that casket—safe, dark, motionless, airless—it will change. It will not be broken; it will become unbreakable, impenetrable, irredeemable. The only place outside of Heaven where you can be perfectly safe from all the dangers and perturbations of love is Hell."[41] To love at all is to be vulnerable—to God and the things that break His heart.

Women love fiercely and intentionally because Jesus first loved us.

There is an ancient tradition that women have celebrated for thousands of years. Wherever there has been cause for joy, there has been henna. They have discovered henna on

---

41. C. S. Lewis, *Four Loves* (New York: Mariner Books, 1971), 121.

the hands of Egyptian mummies from five thousand years ago.[42] In the Middle East and in parts of Africa, women gather to celebrate weddings with henna tattoos. In fact, history tells us that almost all groups of women where henna grows naturally use it to express joy, blessing, and beauty. The most common henna design is a lotus blossom, which represents the awakening of the human soul. It symbolizes grace, beauty, creativity, sensuality, femininity, and purity. In short, henna marks joy on women's bodies.

What better way to celebrate Ella's becoming a woman than a henna night with the women of our family? Though her period had not yet begun, it would soon, and we wanted to welcome her to the company of our women. I also wanted to re-create the symbolism of Anita Diamant's *The Red Tent.* Diamant imagines biblical times in which the large extended family lived in tent villages while their sheep roamed the hills. Once a month, all women of age would share their cycle and convene in the "red tent" for several days. It was a purely feminine time of resting from chores, sharing the intimacy of the woman's period, and passing along traditions, stories, and heritage. This is where a girl truly became a woman. Historically documented or not, I love the picture of this tradition.

While we couldn't re-create a red tent, nor are the women of my family able to talk so candidly about intimate things, I wanted to match the vibe: women of the family celebrating their daughters. I bought Ella a new red shirt and a matching scarf and we borrowed the empty house of my mom's friend one evening when we were all together. We had prepared chocolate fondue, stories, funky music, and special gifts. What we had no way of knowing is that this

---

42. Thomas Joseph Pettigrew, *A History of Egyptian Mummies: And an Account of the Worship and Embalming of the Sacred Animals by the Egyptians* (London: Cambridge University Press, 2013), 66.

friend's lamps all had red shades and her living room furniture was red! We entered a red-cast room and the ambience was complete.

Henna nights are nights of celebration—of storytelling, music, eating, and transitioning. Usually, girls are married the next day. So we created a party for ourselves. A celebration of Ella. We told stories of how we had loved fiercely. We ate an entire bowl of melted chocolate. We drank sparkling grape juice. And we decorated each other's hands and forearms with increasingly elaborate henna designs. We learned how talented my Honduran sister-in-law is with loops and dots and a little more of her love story with my brother. My sister shared how challenging becoming a mother had been but how much her kids had taught her about loving well through patience and grace. My mom shared examples of mothers she worked with as a family worker, about how fiercely they loved their children.

We each had a special gift for Ella—something significant for her to remember how loved she is by her family, by each of us. For as we emerged from our "red tent," we emerged as sisters. And Ella was one of us.

It is just the three of us girls at home the night we watch *Soul Surfer*, the story of Bethany Hamilton's shark attack and subsequent loss of a limb. As an athletic girl, Ella responds well to stories of strength and courage. I have wondered what lesson would emerge from this teenage story of overcoming pain and loss. We watch the buildup: surfing is her family's passion. They all love it, her parents used to be competitive, and Bethany's entire life revolves around the sport. When the loss of her arm throws her off balance on the board, she experiences her whole life equally thrown off kilter. Sometimes, when you love so hard without a greater focus, that very love can destroy you.

After a humbling trip to tsunami-wrecked Thailand, Bethany comes out of her self-absorbed depression. When she surfs again, it is out of genuine passion. And this time, her fans can tell. Letters pour in from handicapped kids all over the world. She inspires them. She realizes her love of surfing, when focused beyond itself, blesses others and gives them hope.

There is something to this. I feel the weight of what we're learning in Bethany's story. We saw it when we watched the ski documentary, *Pretty Faces*. Produced and filmed by female skiers to document their world and inspire young girls to pursue the sport, it illustrates the beauty of doing what you love in a supportive community and for a bigger purpose. The various women who took part in the film were all skilled and passionate skiers, yet they did not tell the story of their individual ability. They went in search of the awesome faces of the mountain they could tackle with each other. In sisterhood, they skied to inspire their younger sisters. We could feel the arc of this desire even as it went unspoken.

When women love fiercely with the support of other women and for the sake of others, an intense beauty and powerful capacity for good is unleashed. Mountains move.

If there is a Mother Teresa for Ella's generation, it may be Katie Davis. Whereas the devoted Albanian Catholic gave her life to India's poor and died before my daughter was born, Katie's story is accessible: a teen who self-admittedly had the cute shoes, cute boyfriend, and cute convertible but was wrecked by Jesus. By the time she was twenty, Katie had adopted nine little girls while starting a ministry in a village in Uganda. In her challenging days, she writes, "I keep stopping and loving one person at a time. Because this is my call as a Christian. I can do only what one woman can do, but I will do what I can. Daily, the Jesus who wrecked my life enables me to do so much more than I ever thought possible."[43]

When Jesus wrecks our lives, he tends to give us the vision and capacity for what he has in mind. I've experienced several wreckings in my years of walking with him. When Khalil showed up in my office two years after the late night "Call to Prayer" letter, prayer blanket in one hand, Holy Koran in the other, I knew this was part of my story. As we began our coworker relationship I came face-to-face with Islam and a passion began to percolate from within to learn more of this mysterious thing that absorbed Khalil. One thing led to another, and my husband and I quit our jobs in Chicago for missions in the Middle East. It didn't matter that I couldn't even say "hello" when we first stepped off the plane for our initial one-year assignment in Turkey. Adventure waited in this ancient city. The Muslim call to prayer woke us at 5 a.m. from the mosques' minarets that dotted the skyline. I was wrecked.

We stayed on and off for ten years, out of love for the Turkish people. When we returned to the States to regroup and go to graduate school, Jesus wrecked me again. I was catching up on what the church cared about, filling in knowledge gaps with trends I had missed. A friend suggested I watch *Born into Brothels*, a film about the sex industry in Kolkata, India, and I spent the night sobbing on our couch, alone in the dark, devastated by what I was learning. That night delineated before and after: I could not continue on as normal with the knowledge of human trafficking. My heart ached for those trapped in sexual exploitation and I had to respond.

Katie Davis writes, "I believe we were each created to change the world for *someone*. To serve *someone*. To love

---

43. Katie Davis, *Kisses from Katie: A Story of Relentless Love and Redemption* (New York: Howard Books, 2011), xix.

someone the way Christ first loved us, to spread his light."[44] Her someones are Ugandan children. She "quit life" to live with them, mother them, care for them and hundreds of others who were in need of food, water, medicine, and love. "The same God created all of us for a purpose, which is to serve Him and to love and care for His people. It is universal. We can't do it in our own strength or out of our own resources, but as we follow God to wherever He is leading us, He makes the impossible happen."[45]

I have friends who have discovered they were created to love through adoption, through making art, serving in their church, through writing and speaking, through using their skills in company jobs that provide for their families, through funding kingdom work, through teaching, through painstakingly caring for the sick or wounded, through staying home to raise little ones, through moving overseas and working in jungles or helping refugees or taking care of the disabled or teaching pastors...my list could go on for pages and pages!

Women are called to love someone the way Christ first loved us, but it will play itself out in as myriad ways as there are sisters on earth.

Ruth and Naomi

Ruth's someone was Naomi.

Their story begins tragically. Fleeing from famine, Naomi's family leaves the land of Judah to settle in Moab, a foreign land with foreign gods. After her husband dies, her two sons each marry Moabite women, strictly forbidden for God's people. Ten years later, they both die, presumably at a young age and as a result of disobeying God on two counts.

---

44. Ibid., xx.
45. Ibid., 95.

My heart goes out to Naomi! One commentator goes so far as to compare her to Job.

Though broken, widowed, and childless, Naomi resolves to return to her homeland. Her strength is admirable, as I can only imagine the journey at her age, but at some point along the way, she changes her mind and implores her daughters-in-law to turn back home. She thinks she can do it alone? Imagine the scene: they are on a rocky, mountainous desert road. They've passed carcasses and overheard rumors of bandits. They know this is no place for women traveling alone. Naomi is wearied, from age and heartbreak. The girls are still young, too young. Every man they pass takes too much notice. Out of great love (we'll believe this over stubbornness), Naomi frees the girls: *Go back to your homeland, your gods, and your families. Remarry and find happiness. Don't follow me to a death sentence.*

Love meets love. Ruth replies back with equal intensity, "Don't urge me to leave you or to turn back from you. Where you go I will go, and where you stay I will stay. Your people will be my people and your God my God. Where you die I will die, and there I will be buried. May the Lord deal with me ever so severely if anything but death separates you and me."[46] It is done. They will remain at each other's side. And Ruth lives up to her proclamation; she continues to love Naomi by working hard in the fields and honoring her reputation. Boaz says, "I've been told all about what you have done for your mother-in-law since the death of your husband—how you left your father and mother and your homeland and came to live with a people you did not know before."[47]

Ruth goes on to marry Boaz and provide a surrogate son for Naomi. The women of the town say, "Praise be to the Lord, who this day has not left you without a kinsman-

---

46. Ruth 1:16–17 (NIV).
47. Ruth 2:11 (NIV).

redeemer. May he become famous throughout Israel! He will renew your life and sustain you in your old age. For your daughter-in-law, who loves you and who is better to you than seven sons, has given him birth."[48] It is said that Naomi cared for him and raised him as her own, but we know Ruth is the mother of Obed, Grandfather to David, in the line of the Messiah. I'd say he became famous in Israel. And it was because Ruth's someone to love was Naomi.

Let us pray our daughters will love as Ruth loved: herself, God, and others. That she will find her *someones* like Katie Davis and in fierce intentionality, change the world through her love.

Ella's Experience

Ella and her dad share a love of hiking. They have more endurance and lung strength than the rest of us and would keep going on almost every family hike we ever attempt. A few years ago they began a tradition of hiking a fourteener every summer. We Coloradoans use that term to describe the fifty-eight mountain peaks that reach fourteen thousand feet in our state. Plenty of natives make it their life's goal to summit all fifty-eight. My daughter is one of them.

During the summer of *Becoming*, they pulled out the back seats of our van and drove up to the trailhead the night before. At the crack of dawn, they peeled off sleeping bags and loaded up on protein-packed oatmeal. The air was brisk and blissfully quiet: all the other cars were vacant as the other hikers had started before dawn. They had one goal other than to summit the mountain: enjoy each other while doing something they equally loved.

Not all of us enjoy hiking to that degree. In fact, some

---

48. Ruth 4:14–15 (NIV).

of you live in areas where a "hike" is more like a long walk through cornfields or a labored trek along a sandy beach. Some might consider a "hike" a steep climb up Seattle's streets or the length of Central Park or an hour on the StairMaster. In fact, when you think of doing something you love with someone you love, some of you aren't even remotely close to thinking about physical exertion. Perhaps a Broadway show comes to mind? A trip to the nail salon? An afternoon at a bookstore? The latest *Star Wars* movie?

When it comes to *Women Love*, there are three things that I imagine Ella must learn: women love because He first loved us; women love best in community; and women love someone (or someplace or something) with fierce intentionality. For her and her dad, they see these three come together most vibrantly on a trail in the mountains. There is no greater love language for them than God's breath in the rustling of the aspens or a mountain goat sighting or the challenge of scaling a boulder field (as if God placed it there on purpose, to delight them!). They will extend this love to others in a father-daughter base camp they are cocreating. Ella will serve as a junior leader for girls ages ten to twelve. I think it's important to recognize the ways God shows us love as the evidence of his wooing. For it is in response to his wooing that we are wrecked for loving others.

Being wrecked is not always fun, nor easy. As C. S. Lewis warned, there is no safe investment. We offer a piece of ourselves when we give it away. Whether that piece is security, comfort, or predictability. Even loving ourselves can prove to be one of the toughest things of living well. Thankfully, there is no greater love than this: He gave up His life for us, His friends.[49]

God of wreckage, disruption, and displacement, stir
in the hearts of this mom and child to discover

---

49. See John 15:13.

their someone, someplace, and something and love fiercely, intentionally, radically.

Questions for you:

1. How has Jesus wrecked you? Can you think of an experience of being wrecked?

2. Who were you created to change the world for? Who is your someone to love? To serve?

3. If your daughter does not yet know she is deeply loved by Jesus, what sort of conversation can you have with her to help her understand?

4. In what ways do you see your daughter loving? What do you already see in her that might wink at her future?

Books for Her to Read	Books I'm Reading	Scripture	Films to Watch	Activities	Gift
Kisses from Katie by Katie	*Jesus Feminist* by Sarah Bessey	Ruth	*Pretty Faces*	Henna Night with Gamma and Aunt Casey and Aunt Gissela	My 13th bday gold ring
	The Red Tent by Anita Diamant	1 John 4:7–21	*Soul Surfer*	Hike a fourteener with Dad	
	For the Love by Jen Hatmaker				

Books for Her to Read	Books I'm Reading	Scripture	Films to Watch	Activities	Gift

8

Women Fight

How hard she is willing to fight for something is a
good indicator of how passionate she is about it.
—Kate Conner[50]

One of my closest friends has lived on my same street for
the last eight years...in two different states. We first met at
church when we moved to Seattle from Turkey and she cud-
dled my screaming toddler in the nursery until she fell asleep
in her arms. It was the first church service I had attended
since my daughter's birth fifteen months prior. Later, we
learned that we lived down the street from each other. When
we moved to Colorado, her family followed a year later and
moved down the street again. Jess is opposite of me in so
many ways: she's a tiny little thing, loves numbers, hates to
cook, has southern belle charm, but writes blunt and task-y
emails, buys loads of concert tickets if left alone too long,
and has an insatiable sweet tooth. I love her.

Ella surpassed Jess in shoe size and height quite some time
ago. So, to see these two practicing self-defense moves on each

50. Kate Conner, *Enough: 10 Things We Should Be Telling Teenage Girls*
(Nashville, TN: B&H Publishing, 2014), 92.

other was a riot. The three of us joined a Gracie Jiu-Jitsu Women Empowered class to kick off the season of Women Fight in *Becoming*. I wanted to do something fun around this topic and also learn some stuff I should have learned decades ago. To think of the places I've been without an ounce of knowledge of how to get out of dicey situations is scary and embarrassing. The few that instantly pop into mind involve getting turned around on the El in Chicago my first year in college, at night, and ending up in an area I should not have been; naively knocking on doors on the West Side of Chicago for my first social work job, ignorant of the gang activity on the street; flying alone back to Turkey after living there (no biggie), transferring to a domestic flight (no biggie), having a friend pick me up and put me on a bus to a village (questionable) at night (bordering on stupid) bound for a pickup point in the middle of the countryside to stay in the home of strangers (insanity). I should have taken self-defense years and years ago!

In the process of *Becoming*, the goal was not for Ella to learn how to truly fight. Joining thirty women in a fun and practical course on how to protect ourselves was meant to launch the conversation: How do women fight for what they believe in?

I am an activist. There's something that feels a little repugnant about that word, like I should wear Birkenstocks and have picket line posters in my trunk and be generally a little bit wild and a tad bit crazy. For a while, I tried to think of myself as an advocate. That sounded better. Who doesn't want to be advocated for? Advocates are nice-looking folks who frequent courtrooms and pass through metal detectors without concern while the activists are kept at bay and sometimes assigned a personal security detail to watch over them. Living fully into who I am as an activist has come slowly.

But let me tell you a story. When I was in fourth grade, I wrote a book, *How to Train Your Parents*, for all ten-year-olds struggling with mom and dad (not yet published). In high school, I spoke in front of the school board about removing inappropriate magazines from our library. In my first year in college, I joined a group of nuns on a bus and drove from Chicago to D.C. to march to the Capitol on the twentieth anniversary of *Roe v. Wade*. The next year, I wrote a letter to everyone I knew telling them about children growing up in poverty in Chicago and imploring them to pray. In my first job after graduation, I worked with foster children in poor families on the West Side of Chicago. A year later, I convinced my husband that the most useful way to spend our lives was to reach the unreached in the largest unreached nation in the world.

Ahem. We might call me a wee bit passionate. But let me ask, do you hear the theme? I didn't. For so long. Years after convincing my husband to move to the largest unreached nation, I found myself tired, burned out, and disillusioned trying to talk about Jesus to the bored, privileged Turkish students lucky enough to be at university. I felt lost and adrift and wondered why. I had forgotten my story. Lost the plot. Stopped authoring and stopped acting because I was living the wrong script. Only by leaving was I able to remember my narrative, the theme of my story: *I am an activist.*

And activists need to fight for what they care about. They need to fight to see their passion fulfilled and realized. The passion may change, but the need to collaborate with God to bring His kingdom to earth as it is in heaven does not. The question is: What aspect of Jesus' heart breaks yours? Founding a nonprofit seeking to reframe the marginalized with dignity was natural for me. Advocating for anti–human trafficking was natural. Because this is how I reveal God: *by caring for those the world has harmed.*

Not all women are activists, but I believe all women have a fighting instinct. Isn't this what *mama bear* refers to? That moment when someone or something comes against our children and that primal, instinctual reflex takes over: protect at all cost. We all have our loves and passions that we will naturally fight for. These are the things we willingly sacrifice time and money to see change. What is your thing? Have you even identified it yet? Dan Allender writes, "It's a choice, just as in *The Matrix*, between the red pill and the blue pill. One will quiet you and let you sleep through the terror of this world, while the other will awaken you to be a warrior fueled by the passions of redemption."[51]

What are you willing to fight for?

My friend Jenni wants to go to Afghanistan almost as much as I do. She belongs to a large church that regularly sends teams to nurture the relationships with a NGO they support. My interest in the country began when the Taliban covered all the women in burkas and is similar to my insatiable curiosity about the Iranian Revolution, the Berlin Wall during the Cold War, and Jewish ghettos in Europe. I am fascinated by what happens to a people under oppression. When I read of the resiliency of humanity, the courage of women, and the rebellion of artists under repressive regimes, I am full of hope. They become my heroes.

So Jenni and I, both photographers, took Ella to watch *Frame by Frame*, the story of four Afghan photojournalists dedicated to telling a truthful story about Afghanistan. Under Taliban rule, photography was banned. A conservative reading of the Koran suggests that a photographic image of Allah's creation supposes equality with him. To be seen with

---

51. Dan Allender, *To Be Told* (Colorado Springs: WaterBrook Press, 2005), 70.

a camera during those years meant death. With the Taliban gone for now, photojournalism is flourishing in Afghanistan. Farzana was one of the featured photographers in the documentary and we watched her fight to tell the true story of her fellow women.

One story stood out. Farzana was trying to document the devastating trend of female acid attacks. After unsuccessfully interviewing women in Herat, one of the worst regions for this practice, Farzana was able to talk with one brave woman. Cloaked by a veil and eyes downcast, she shares that she was engaged at age six and married off at age eleven. The groom and his family were abusive, including during her pregnancy. Soon after the birth of her first child, the father-in-law threw acid on her face and lit a match while her husband stood by laughing. He offered to grant her a divorce so long as he kept her child. Farzana and this courageous young woman tell her story together, through photographs and an interview, in an effort to educate their country and outside forces to these atrocities.

Farzana fights for what she believes in with her camera lens, her weapon of choice. She is reframing Afghanistan: "If a country is without photography, that country is without an identity."[52] And she has had to ask herself, "If I die, is it worth it?" To not be worthless again, Farzana believes it is. All of it.

There is another woman I want my daughter to know: Donaldina Cameron, a Scottish-American missionary in the early 1900s, who fought to free more than three thousand Chinese sex slaves from brothels in San Francisco. By now, Ella's literacy teacher must be wondering. After finishing *Kisses*

---

52. *Frame by Frame*, directed and produced by Alexandria Bombach and Mo Scarpelli, 2015.

from Katie, she brought *Fierce Compassion* to class. Her explanation was not enough to dismiss the confused, but intrigued, look on her teacher's face so she said, "My mom gives me homework." Oh, I can't wait for parent-teacher conferences!

Fierce Compassion, researched and written by a mother/daughter team, brings to life the work of an early abolitionist left out of history books. After teaching for a year at the mission house in San Francisco, she returned for four decades to rescue and restore Chinese women. She gave up marriage and family to be mother to the girls out of her great love for God. In one impassioned speech she rallied, "Our talents are diverse, our opportunities differ, our pathways in life diverge, but our Master's call to service is the same to all. All fields are his and the promise is unfailing and the command is explicit."[53]

When I started taking anti–human trafficking more seriously, my kids were much younger. The box of books would arrive and I immediately hid them from view. The bus pulled up out front and off went YouTube or the Netflix documentary I'd been watching. I talked vaguely about helping people who were made to do things they didn't want to do. And then, slowly, as they grew, I began to share age-appropriate stories with them. And my passion oozed. To date, all three of my kids have chosen to do papers or projects on modern-day slavery. They have been turned down by teachers and have received odd looks from peers because they have begun to care deeply about what I care about, like it or not.

My mom is also a passionate woman. These days, though retired and playing an inordinate amount of golf and Pickle-

---

53. Kristen and Kathryn Wong, *Fierce Compassion* (Michigan: New Earth Enterprises, 2012), 131.

ball, she is studying about Alzheimer's and volunteers in a respite facility. When I was growing up, she worked for Head Start and helped start a public school version of early childhood intervention. I remember how close she was to "her families." I remember buying our used cars from Junior and running into people who knew her all over town. They loved her. Was she not the one who removed economic barriers for me? Helped me treat marginalized people with dignity? Gave me a vision for caring for those the world has harmed?

The role of a mom is invaluable. We shape our daughters as they watch us. My girls may not take up the banner of fighting human trafficking, but I want them to be passionate enough about something that they're willing to fight with time, money, and sacrifice to see it changed. In the meantime, Ella may not be able to read a book about her mom, but she can read about women like her mom. I want her to respect what I do and understand why I do it. I want her to have a high opinion of me so that the way I live my life can be emulated. If I expect her to fight for what she believes in, she better see me doing just that.

In my search for resources for moms like me, I have found a voice I resonate with, and want to drill over coffee for hours. Kate Conner, author of *Enough* and the viral blog post "10 Things We Should Be Telling Teenage Girls," gets what I'm going for in this new way of ushering girls into womanhood. Her perspective is raw, authentic, and so refreshingly relevant. In a chapter addressing relational drama, she offers a cure so brilliant and obvious I've literally walked around the house saying, "Yes!" out loud while fist-bumping the air. Listen: "Our souls need passion and purpose. When we can't find it authentically, we manufacture it in the form of drama and daydreams to feed our hungry hearts. The problem is that a woman subsisting off of drama and daydreams is like a lion subsisting off of grass, berries, and bugs. We might survive, but we will never be healthy, and we will never be satisfied."[54] The cure to teen drama? Passion.

Give me a woman still feeding on drama and gossip, depressed by her own boredom, and helicoptering over children because of a misplaced identity and I'll give you a woman living a small story. These are the women who say things like, "Our girls are missing out because they haven't had a mani-pedi yet." Oh yes, I've been told this. Is it feasible that these very women are raising girls who also feed on drama? Girls who in their lack of passion and purpose will run to other things to fill the heart hunger?

We are designed for so much more. Dan Allender, in the way only he can articulate, says "It matters little what problem, population, or place you tackle. It only matters that something in your soul pulses with eternity to join the cast of characters that ventures to create glory and beauty out of the ashes of the Fall."[55] Our aim in life is to discover our story and the way in which we are to collaborate with God to bring heaven to earth. And our daughters, right in the midst of self-discovery, need help beginning to name the passions that fuel their narrative. Conner encourages them to pay attention to what makes them cry. It is a clue to the thing in Jesus' heart that breaks theirs.

When our daughters are exposed to the "ashes of the Fall" in conjunction with an imagination and an expectation to create beauty out of it, passion and purpose will fill the hungry heart. Why? Because we were designed to fight for

---

54. Kate Conner, *Enough: 10 Things We Should Be Telling Teenage Girls* (Nashville, TN: B&H Publishing, 2014), 71.

55. Dan Allender, *To Be Told* (Colorado Springs: Water Brook Press, 2005), 70.

what we believe in. I call it passionate resistance. We must resist injustice and evil to expose God's glory.

Conner nails it: "Crack the door and let all of the broken, beautiful humanity flood in like a sunbeam. Let it in; let it move her. Let it inspire her, wreck her, challenge her. Let it change her. If you want her to catch the fire, you're going to have to put her near a flame."[56] Girls on a mission to stop human trafficking don't have time for drama. Girls dedicated to eradicating dating violence don't have time for drama. Girls raising money to support girls' education in Uganda don't have time for drama. They are living for a bigger story rather than consumed by a myopic vision for themselves. Honestly, they are too busy fighting.

We are walking toward the event and I feel compelled to coach her. To remind her not to use her "toddler voice" with the families we'll serve today. I imagine courageous faces, overcoming pride and maybe covering shame, to come and receive services. She will need to treat them as equals, not the poor. I tell her. We are arm in arm, headed to a low-income clothing and service event. It's an attempt to wreck and challenge her. I wonder if she'll cry. Tears are signs I'm on the lookout for.

Of course, fighting to end poverty, or homelessness, or lack of education, or immigration rights, or any number of "issues" represented today, might not be Ella's story. And perhaps what we're supposed to see at this event are examples of other women fighting for what they believe in. I don't mean the staff or volunteers; I mean the mamas who dragged their kiddos out at 8 a.m. on this Saturday morning. The

---

56. Kate Conner, *Enough: 10 Things We Should Be Telling Teenage Girls* (Nashville, TN: B&H Publishing, 2014), 82.

mama we spend an hour with, communicating via her eleven-year-old daughter, looking for shoes that fit the boys and a coat in purple for Sayeda, our little translator. A mama who already knows about all the services and doesn't need dental care or eye checkups because she is already on top of it for her tribe. Whose story we can't possibly learn but in whose eyes we see clearly: she is strong and loving. She fights for a good life for her family.

After we escort two families through the maze of social services and clothing, Ella joins her friend with all the other kids at the carnival, waits in line for snow cones, wins tickets at the fair games for a prize. She is one of them. No different. This humanity, that we are all the same, whether we speak different languages, sleep on couches or beds, or wear new or used clothes, is a beautiful thing. Sometimes you fight with a determination and it looks like survival, and it takes more effort than any of my human-trafficking presentations. Sayeda's mama is added to my list of heroes.

Tabitha's Story

One woman is referred to as a disciple in the New Testament, though we know many more followed Jesus and were a part of the apostle entourage. Tabitha lived in the port city of Joppa and was "always doing good and helping the poor."[57] When she became ill and died, the disciples heard that Peter was in the nearby town of Lydda and sent for him to come at once. They had washed and prepared her body in the upper room, indicating she was a woman of means. Perhaps she was a benefactor of the church in Joppa much like Lydia and Phoebe. If this was the case, she used her wealth to care for

---

57. Acts 9:36 (NIV).

the poor and widows, as they were all hovering around her when Peter arrived and shooed them out.[58]

Here was a well-loved woman who cared for those who might have been different, even Gentile. The fact that Luke, author of Acts, includes her Greek name, Dorcas, may indicate that she was well known to Gentile believers in Joppa. And the fact that Peter walked from Lydda to Joppa to attend to this female disciple says she was well loved by Jesus' followers, maybe even knowing Jesus Himself. She was a fighter worth fighting for and they were unwilling to lose her.

That Tabitha is included in early church history is no small thing. I dare say she was a passionate woman who fought for widows with her time, skill, and wealth.

Ella's Experience

Ella's social studies teacher is awesome. Having come from teaching college and high school, he not only has high expectations, but he knows the importance of real-life application to the study topics. So in seventh grade, he had his students create a nonprofit. If they finished assignments, they were rewarded by computer lab time to create a website, or team planning for fund-raisers, or other such small groups that divided the workload of forming a little social advocacy program. The biggest challenge: agree upon an issue to support.

You know where this is going. Ella had joined me at one of my human-trafficking presentations a month prior and left even more concerned about a particular classmate who seemingly had many of the risk factors I described. In lieu of having yet identified her own "thing," she knew my thing was a pretty big thing. She began to lobby for anti–human trafficking among her peers and convinced her teacher this

---

58. Acts 9:39 (NIV).

was a worthy cause. He cyber-stalked my organization and eventually the entire seventh grade agreed their nonprofit should benefit anti-trafficking work. As if that weren't cool enough, her teacher invited me to spend an entire day training every single seventh and eighth grader at the school to understand the signs of trafficking and learn action steps to take.

As in everything, we rarely know the impact our actions have, but Ella's fight to champion something she knew was important might protect another kid from horrendous exploitation. I've shared before that I have no expectations that she will develop a passion for what I'm passionate about, though I think this shows the inevitable contagion to daughter if mom is excited about something. She has tasted and seen what it means to fight for what you believe in. Passion and purpose have begun to fill her hungry heart.

In the years that follow, my hope is that these experiences will form a template for her. If God has designed women to fight, what does she imagine that to look like? Does it come in the form of civil disobedience the way the British suffragists were portrayed in the film *Suffragette*? If, after fighting for fifty years through peaceful discourse, a basic right was still denied, what would *you* do? Does it come in the form of risking one's life? Donaldina Cameron snuck slaves out of San Francisco brothels at risk to all of their lives yet counted it worth it. What is our measure to evaluate what's worth it? Does it come in the form of strong, loud women who fight for noble causes in a manner of something to prove? What attitude does a godly fighting woman comport?

The Bible tells us to act justly, love mercy, and walk humbly with God.[59] We are also told to think on "whatever is true, whatever is noble, whatever is right, whatever

---

59. Micah 6:8 (NIV).

is lovely, whatever is admirable—if anything is excellent or praiseworthy—think about such things."[60] And we are given an example to follow in Christ, "Who, being in very nature God did not consider equality with God something to be grasped, but made himself nothing, taking the very nature of a servant, being made in human likeness. And being found in appearance as a man, he humbled himself."[61] I don't know about you, but in these verses I see a template of a humble believer committed to truth on behalf of another for the glory of God.

Our souls pulse with eternity. There are casts of characters we get to join as we bring God's kingdom to earth as it is in heaven. As our daughters mature into their narrative, my prayer is that they will fight for beauty to be made from ashes. I pray they will be humble justice seekers filled with a passion worthy of fighting for.

Lord of collaboration, thank You for the privilege of fighting alongside You and the great honor this mom and her daughter have to join You in the story you are telling through them.

Questions for you:

1. What was aroused in you as you read about women and drama and passion? Do you have a passion and purpose? How would you describe it?

2. How have you imparted some of your interests and passions to your daughter already?

---

60. Philippians 4:8 (NIV).
61. Philippians 2:6–8 (NIV).

3. How can you be more intentional about exposing her to things that might inspire her, wreck her, or challenge her?

4. In what ways do you already see your daughter fighting for something she believes in?

Books for Her to Read	Books I'm Reading	Scripture	Movies to Watch	Activities	Gift
Fierce Compassion by Kristin and Kathryn Wong	*Enough* by Kate Conner	Tabitha Acts 9:36–43	*Frame by Frame* with Jenni	Self-defense class with Jess	Necklace with a key to symbolize unlocking your passion, for it tells you what you'll fight for
It's Your World by Chelsea Clinton	*To Be Told* by Dan Allender		*Suffragette*	Children in need event	
	Let's All Be Brave by Annie Downs		*He Named Me Malala*	Youth Prevention Presentation on Human Trafficking by me	
			Lord of the Rings: Return of the King		

Books for Her to Read	Books I'm Reading	Scripture	Films to Watch	Activities	Gift

9

Women Sacrifice

Guide me, if I'm willing
(drive me if I'm not)
into the hard ways of sacrifice
which are just and loving.
—Ted Loder[62]

Ella came down the stairs one night unable to talk. We were sitting on the couch watching TV and she leaned over the cushions sobbing. She has shed more tears this year than her entire post-nonverbal life and it has not gone unnoticed. I have been watching, storing in my heart that which stirs hers to tears, beginning to paint a picture of who she might become, where those tears will lead her.

On this night, we waited long minutes for the heaving, snorting sobs to abate. She held up her book, *Hiding in the Light* by Rifqa Bary, and read the passage that described Rifqa's conversion, the moment she surrendered all to Jesus. Rifqa was a Muslim girl in a conservative Sri Lankan Ohioan family who ultimately sacrificed her culture,

62. Ted Loder, *Guerillas of Grace* (Minneapolis: Augsburg Books, 1981), 106.

family, and safety to follow the still small voice of her Savior. In her book, she chronicles the journey of escape, hiding, and eventual freedom to pursue her faith. It is a powerful story.

Rifqa's testimony is not unlike the multitude of Turkish believers I know or the millions of people around the world responding to dreams, miracles, and the Bible translated in their own language. But it is unlike anything most American girls have experienced. Particularly girls who have grown up in the church. What does Ella know of sacrifice for faith? When has she ever heard of a girl her age willing to trade her own family to follow Jesus?

She read the passage and smiled, acknowledging how impacted she was over Rifqa's journey, how aware she was of what was happening in her own soul. When she went back upstairs, I turned to my husband and gave him a silent high-five. Mission accomplished. Recall the first words of this book. *I am out to wreck my daughter.*

I have been working to break her heart for that which breaks Jesus' heart. Whittling away at the lens that culture has created for girls her age, to give her a new lens through which to view the world. With new sight, she is starting to see the scaffolding we're building. In Rifqa's story she sees: women sacrifice.

I hesitated to choose this category and recognize it needs to be treated with care. How do we raise strong girls to embrace this as a beautiful gift we give to the world, not a call to self-diminishment? In fact, I'm sure many women have already bristled at the word *sacrifice*. Plenty of conservative Christian authors have implored us to serve our children and husbands without even a nod to our own desire. I recall reading one who suggested I refresh my clothes and makeup prior to my husband returning home in the evening so as to best serve his needs that night. Hear me when I say, I do not mean we lose ourselves to that which we sacrifice.

As women, we have had our share of laying aside (either permanently or temporarily) one thing to give ourselves fully to another. There have been many in my life. The one time I could be accused of physically assaulting my then would-be husband was when he asked me to go to a future options kind of conference within our campus ministry. He was seriously considering joining staff and I lacked even the remotest desire. In fact, I felt strongly the opposite and let his shins know it. *But I went and God slowly changed my heart about ministry.*

A few years later, heart significantly changed, I was so excited to finally land at the University of Michigan, after months of raising financial support, and begin campus ministry. We had been married four years and were loving the freedom of life as just the two of us. I fully anticipated the Michigan students to become more friends than disciples. I had so many dreams that when I started to feel uncharacteristically tired, emotional, and tender, I assumed I had a thyroid disease. Disease made more sense to me, because the night my husband bought a pregnancy test and made me take it, I sobbed at the top of the stairs. I was ten weeks pregnant. This did not fit into my current plan. *But God eventually prepared me to yield my body and dreams to motherhood.*

After a few years of parenting, I started to figure out how to combine my passions and gifts while being present to little ones. I began to see how they could simultaneously exist. A few authors were instrumental in my understanding of desire and I wanted to bring one to speak at a women's conference I was helping to host. My supervisor thought otherwise. Disagreeing with these authors, she adamantly opposed my idea. In that moment, I knew I could fight for my opinion, or tread carefully with her heart that was obviously reacting out of an unknown wounding. *Sacrificing my idea to humble myself before her was a spiritual act of honor and respect.*

And this is what I want to impart to my daughter: Women sacrifice as they humble themselves to others (husbands, babies, friends, teammates) without losing their voice.

Ella is the second born with a firstborn personality. Perhaps it is because she is the firstborn girl? She is competitive, ambitious, and organized. She fills a room with her presence. When she was two, she composed her first song, "Ella Walking Up the Hill" and sang it over and over and over again. She has been singing made-up lyrics and memorized favorites loudly and continuously ever since. When not singing, she is recounting her dreams, quoting memes from Pinterest, and generally filling every bit of silence. Needless to say, this is wearisome to the actual firstborn with a third-born personality.

We began to notice the effect of their personalities on each other years ago, and mistakenly focused more on our son's patience, than Ella's noise. Honestly, whenever we said something to her, it felt personal and wounding. We were unsure as to how to help her consider others, particularly in shared space.

My husband drove them both to school and every afternoon, I picked them up. Comparing notes, we had the same experience: in the ramp-up to our son working out what to say, Ella usually filled the space and he retreated to silence, not eager enough to talk that he was willing to battle his sister. When this same phenomenon began to ooze into the dinner table, we hatched a plan.

We love her voice. It is a beautiful symbol of what we wanted the *Becoming* year to accomplish—find your voice and offer it to the world. But what would it look like to sacrifice something so natural and even so lovely, for the sake of another, while still maintaining the fullness of herself, her gifts, and her passion? What would it look like to choose silence, to make room for her older brother to find his own voice?

In the wee hours of one morning, before the ride to school, Ella and her dad had a talk. She was reading Rifqa's story and learning about sacrifice, but what in *her* life might require a little bit of sacrifice? Was there anything she might lay aside for the sake of someone else, to humble herself before another by choice and service, rather than force and resentment? It only took a little guiding to arrive at our desired outcome. She knew she overwhelmed the space she and her brother occupied. Perhaps right now, her greatest sacrifice would be her own voice in the car rides to and from school?

The art of becoming is a layered process mixed with rather small life lessons and adjustments alongside meta-narratives. Sometimes we sacrifice an idea, sometimes our very lives. Where have you been called to humble yourself before another?

Irena Sendler and Corrie ten Boom. These are the kind of women you wonder if you're remotely similar to. If given the same time period, the same circumstances, would your faith hold up? Would your heart for justice prevail? Would you stand up to tyranny and evil and sacrifice your own safety to do good, love mercy, and walk humbly with the Lord?

I wonder if I would have the resolve to sneak around Nazi soldiers to secure food rations, false identity papers, and later children, crying babies, and fearful human beings. Perhaps this is why I love reading about Irenas and Corries. Their courage tests my own, prepares me in some ways. Perhaps if I consider the risks, weigh the consequences, and steel my faith, I'll choose similarly. Perhaps one day I'll be counted among the heroines of sacrifice.

Irena fell into obscurity after the war, partially because Poland fell to the communist regime of the Soviet Union, and it was not until a group of students in a Kansas high school turned their research into a play that she gained recognition. The students wrote the screenplay, *Life in a Jar*, in 1999 that was produced two hundred times and turned into a film in 2009. It tells the story of the Polish Catholic who used her social work position checking for typhus in the Warsaw Ghetto to smuggle 2,500 children to safety. She wrote each name and their resettlement location on a slip of paper she placed in a jar. Her hope was to reunify the children with their families after the war.

At the time, Poland was the only German-occupied country with a death sentence to anyone (and their entire family) caught aiding Jews. In 1943, Irena was arrested, severely beaten, and sentenced to death by firing squad, but the Jewish resistance helped her escape. After the war, she was imprisoned and beaten again, this time causing premature labor, which led to the death of her firstborn.

Ella and I watched the film, *The Courageous Heart of Irena Sendler* and came face-to-face with the evil of Hitler. She had never witnessed such unexplainable racism and had a hard time grasping the Jewish genocide. Irena's willingness to sacrifice her own life for the lives of helpless children was extraordinary. It begged the question, what would we do?

A few days later, we watched *The Hiding Place*. Corrie ten Boom was a Dutch Christian, compelled by her faith to smuggle as many Jews to safety as she could. She and her father and sister quietly built a wall in her bedroom, creating a secret room, and their home became part of an underground railroad for Jewish neighbors. Eventually, it was too risky to secure passage and six Jews and resistance workers remained in the ten Boom house. Corrie sacrificed her bedroom, her privacy, and her family, for they were eventually betrayed and imprisoned and her father and sister died in the concentration camps.

On a minuscule level, Ella could relate. Two years earlier, she gave up her room for a young teenage girl to stay with us for a month. Coming from a home with substance and verbal abuse and extreme poverty, our guest numbed the pain by cutting, overmedicating, and talking with men online. She came with trash bags full of clothes reeking of smoke, a stench that remained for months after she left despite wide open windows, fans, air freshener, and hot soapy water.

What felt significant at the time, took on even more meaning as we hung it upon the scaffolding of women sacrifice. Ella had rubbed shoulders with the strength of some of our heroines. The same thing that compelled Corrie to sacrifice her room (and life) for those in need coursed through Ella's veins: an intuitive desire to act justly, love mercy, and walk humbly with God. We named it. *Women reflect God's glory as they offer themselves to others.*

Ann Voskamp writes, "In naming that which is right before me, that which I'd otherwise miss, the invisible becomes visible."[63] What is of such importance to our beliefs, our values, and our passion that we will sacrifice everything to bring it about? That which lies in secret, in the hidden places of our soul, becomes visible when we name. Rifqa sacrificed her family for faith. Jesus was worth it. Irena sacrificed her body (and her own unborn child) for Jewish children. Protecting the innocent was worth it.

Women sacrifice. In myriad small, seemingly insignificant ways and loud, public, heroic sorts of ways. We sacrifice our bodies to bring forth life, stretch marks an eternal reminder

---

63. Ann Voskamp, *One Thousand Gifts* (Nashville, TN: Zondervan, 2011), 54.

of how we yield to the person growing within. We sacrifice bank accounts and emotional reserves for every child brought home through adoption. We sacrifice in marriage and friendship, in careers and for charities.

The question for most women is not *Do you sacrifice?*, but rather when you sacrifice, *Are you maintaining your voice?* We lay our lives down daily, willingly or not. But when we humble ourselves to another, we must do so in a manner that preserves our voice, that is, our sense of self in its fullness. The resolve with which we act, offer, serve, reserve, decline, and so forth. It stems from a reservoir of character and conviction. Perhaps we could call it our essential self, as Shauna Niequist writes about.

Shauna's *Present Over Perfect* is part memoir, part manifesto about the recovery of her voice, which she sacrificed to everyone else's definition of what was good and right for her. She writes, "I knew so well, so deeply that the areas in which my life went off course were the same areas in which I had abdicated responsibility and voice. I did what 'people' thought would be good for me. I did what 'should' have been done. I became what I was 'expected' to become."[64] The only true life-giving sacrifice comes from internal forces, not external expectations.

Sacrifice is a movement of intentional strength to yield life.

Women at Wells

We return to Hagar. Sweet girl at the well. Did you know her name means "sojourner"? Recall that she has fled mistreatment from her mistress, Sarai, and is on the desert road to Shur when the angel of the Lord finds her. Pregnant,

---

64. Shauna Niequist, *Present Over Perfect* (Nashville, TN: Zondervan, 2016), 201.

alone, abused, the Lord *sees* her. They share an intimate moment and she is privileged to bestow the name *El Roi* upon the God of the universe.

What He asks of her is no joke. Having heard her cry for help, the Lord asks her to go back to the suffering, the mistreatment, the status of slave and concubine. He asks her to sacrifice, what? Dignity? Safety? Peace? Family and culture, for was she not on her way back home, to Egypt? Yet even as He tells her to return, He promises a future. I can't help but wonder if the character and conviction she draws upon is for the sake of future descendants, a promise unequaled in Old Testament times. Her voice, the fullness of who she is, will live through the wild donkey of a boy she carries. To this unknown future she humbles herself. To El Roi and his promise.

She names the well *Beer Lahai Roi*, well of the living one who sees me. And as I fast-forward hundreds of years to another woman at a well, I wonder. Did the Samaritan woman call Jesus El Roi? Surely she would have known Hagar's story. Why has she come alone to the well? Is she an outcast? Avoiding shame? She too is *seen* and *promised* something: all who worship in spirit and truth will have a spring of water welling up to eternal life. She need only sacrifice her shame to use her voice and spread the news.

Through two women at wells, many would experience living water. Sacrifice leads to blessing.

Ella's Experience

As the New Year rolled in and kid activities slowed, boring afternoons evolved into elaborate dreaming of bedroom renovation and redecorating. Sketches were drawn. Pinterest boards created. And the two sisters concocted plans for each of their rooms. They both wanted change spanning the spectrum of simple, inexpensive requests to elaborate overhauls. There was no way we were doing it all.

I was in search of an experience Ella and I could share that would focus our eyes on sacrifice. There were plenty of options in our community, but none actually felt sacrificial. Instead, it seemed like we would benefit more than anyone we served. I had ideas such as giving things up in solidarity with the global poor. But again, that felt more like a challenge than a true act of sacrifice for my particular daughter.

When the girls had exhausted their creativity and master maneuvering of us, the pocketbooks, I pulled Ella aside. What would she think of spending a weekend working on her sister's room instead of her own? It would be incredibly difficult to forego her own plans and dreams and focus that same energy (and money) on her sister instead. I couldn't think of a better metaphor for women sacrifice. And she agreed.

The greatest joys in life often come from unexpected twists and turns in our well-thought-out plans. Mostly, it involves yielding a bit of ourselves for the sake of someone else. Sometimes, it requires an even larger sacrifice for that which is right and true. But it always works best when we humble ourselves. Let us begin by searching our soul for that resolve, that place of deep character and conviction out of which our truest self chooses to sacrifice out of humility. Let us tend to the reservoir. Is it empty? Low? Leaking? Let us tend to the source so that our offering is pure. So that our voice is steady.

God of big asks, who asked a virgin teen to carry the holy son and that very beloved to give His life for all, give this mama and her teen the character and conviction to humbly offer themselves in the sacred art of sacrifice.

Questions for you:

1. Have you found it difficult to read this chapter? How do you feel about the idea of sacrifice as a woman? What emotions surfaced as you considered your marriage, parenting, or job?

2. What examples can you share with your daughter?

3. Are there areas of her life where you can foster this idea or orchestrate opportunities to practice humbling herself before another?

4. Do you have a reservoir of character and conviction from which your voice emerges?

Books for Her to Read	Books I'm Reading	Scripture	Films to Watch	Activities	Gift
Hiding in the Light by Rifqa Bary	*The Hardest Peace* by Kara Tippetts	Genesis 16 (Hagar)	*The Courageous Heart of Irena Sendler*	Redecorate sister's bedroom	As a symbol, she gave a gift to her sister, instead of receiving one herself.
	Present Over Perfect by Shauna Niequist	John 4 (Woman at the Well)	*The Hiding Place*	Be silent in the car with her older brother	

Books for Her to Read	Books I'm Reading	Scripture	Films to Watch	Activities	Gift

10

Women Create

This is when art is a verb rather than a noun. It isn't something you point to, it's a way you live.
—Emily P. Freeman[65]

Our last few months in Turkey, I came alive. Perhaps it was the relief that a change was on the horizon. Perhaps it coincided with our last baby sleeping through the night. But I tend to think it is connected to a late-night conversation at our dining room table with a South African therapist named Willie. He flew in from his Paris office to administer an in-depth personality test and go over the results with us. I have no memory of why we did this, nor recall the bulk of the questions, answers, or final assessment. I remember one, singular, number: 99 percent. The number attached to my need to have artistic expression in my work. Boom!

That little number, and Willie's probing questions to understand it, changed my life. For the first time I felt released to be myself. That need to paint every new office space, cook elaborate meals, start a blog, or photograph our

65. Emily P. Freeman, *A Million Little Ways: Uncover the Art You Were Made to Live* (Grand Rapids, MI: Revell, 2013), 105.

team all started to take on meaning. I was a creative. But not just that, I reflected my Creator in every small attempt to bring beauty out of the ordinary. The years of trying to fit into a shape my soul was not designed to fit had taken its toll, yet I had wrongly assumed because it was good and needed, it was what I should do.

The 99 percent validated my desire. It validated my daydreams, journaling, and hobbies. It became an irrefutable fact that I was designed in certain ways, for certain things. And if I was created to express God in these ways, that meant others were designed to express Him in their unique ways. As basic as it sounds, the 99 percent opened my eyes to see, as Emily Freeman says, "I am an image bearer. I have a job to do."[66] (And I wasn't doing it on the mission field.)

We are all image bearers with jobs to do, art to create. Emily's book *A Million Little Ways* is a beautiful exhortation to "embrace the truth of our image-bearing identity and live into the job we've been given to do."[67] She asks, "What full glory does my life labor to reveal?" We were designed to reveal the glory of God. Our life's labor is a process of telling the story of the Creator through his creation in us.

We were made to create, even those of you who don't think you have a "creative" bone in your body. Artists make visible the invisible. They make order out of disorder (accountants). They make technology out of minerals (engineers). They make music out of instruments that were made from wood and horse hair and leather. They make healthy bodies through surgery (doctors). They make families safe by putting out fires and arresting bad guys (firemen and police). They make kids smart by teaching them day after day, for years (teachers). They make scrumptious food from fruits

---

66. Ibid., 69.
67. Ibid., 32.

of the earth (chefs). Do you get what I'm saying? Not only is this what "artists" do, but all of us "*are* art and [we] *make* art."[68]

Eddy and Sandy are artist friends. Eddy weaves words into sermons and Sandy weaves fabric into tapestries. They pastor a small church with big hearts and were very present in my life during the year of *Becoming*. When I started writing, I gathered a stack of church bulletins with scribbles filling every empty space with the thoughts Eddy inspired. I guess he was my pastor muse. Sandy on the other hand was my creative library. A fellow reader, gatherer of ideas, and seeker of depth, she regularly sent me quotes, poems, and helped me sort through big concepts of womanhood. I wonder at her own process of becoming as she journeyed alongside of me and Ella.

Eddy helped me understand that we create life and beauty to make the invisible visible, to declare God at work, to cast our eyes upon a bigger story because we want and need more than what we see. "Living in this world makes us hungry. We crave God with a spiritual hunger. We want more. So the need to create is the craving of God, the desire to worship. *Blessed are the poor because they are hungry*, they're not satisfied." As we live and work in the image of the Creator, artists lift things up and call them holy. Jesus lifted up humanity and declared it holy. Our mandate is to declare the world as it really is: *This is holy. This is a gift.*[69]

I love viewing Sandy's art on display at shows or up close on my screen as I edit the photographs I've taken for her. But beyond her personal art, Sandy loves to help other

---

68. Ibid., 32–33.
69. Eddy Hopkins, Peak Community Church, sermon, May 18, 2014.

women create beauty out of their story. She leads a Reclaiming Remnants workshop for women to deconstruct memories through God's eyes. It was an honor for Ella to spend a day with Sandy for a mini workshop in her studio.

Inviting her into a space full of textiles, rich with color, and abundant in texture Sandy balanced the senses with a quiet, reflective morning. The focus was not on skill, but rather the telling of a new story with repurposed materials. What would emerge from Ella's soul? What story begged to be told that day in the studio? They worked side by side and Sandy occasionally named the metaphors: *How is this like life? How do women create life and beauty out of the ordinary? How do we offer the fullness of ourselves to God's redemptive work?*

I am thankful for Sandy. Thankful that I have a creative friend to back me up in this category. But to be honest, I had a lot of ideas here. Too many. I toyed with the idea of pairing Ella with my police officer friend to witness a woman committed to justice for our city. I thought about having her compose and record a song with our musician friend. I considered having her shadow my professor friend, who teaches a Communications and Human Trafficking class. They all would have been incredible examples to Ella of women creating life and beauty. Ultimately, I chose a friend who had walked with me through the journey and could effortlessly speak the truths I desired to convey.

"Everywhere we go, people breathe in the exquisite fragrance. Because of Christ, we give off a sweet scent rising to God, which is recognized by those on the way to salvation—an aroma redolent with life. But those on the way to destruction treat us more like the stench aroma from a rotting corpse."[70]

---

70. 2 Corinthians 2:15 (MSG).

It makes me think of C. S. Lewis's words, "There are no mere mortals."[71] Every individual is an eternal soul, on the way to salvation or on the way to destruction. The same could be said for our words. There are no meaningless words. They are all either life giving or life sucking even though to some they will all be received as the stench of death.

Ella walks outside during lunch and heads toward her crowd. They are near the same tree, having a familiar conversation. She lingers and listens, though her eyes scan the blacktop. A girl sits alone on the picnic table. The same girl who has been teased as of late in art class. She stood up for her today and it didn't go well. Now, she decides to take it more seriously: she goes to sit next to her. Making the ultimate social statement a middle-schooler can make, she essentially says, "I see you. I value you. I will remove your loneliness."

Later, with a hint of disgust in her voice, one of the tree-standing friends asks her what that was all about. Ella replies, "Don't you feel good sometimes talking to people who are alone or paying attention to kids without many friends?" The friend does not agree. In fact, she responds as if Ella has breathed the stench of death. It is such a pained visceral response that there is nowhere left for the conversation to turn.

Though Ella created a moment of beauty, a space in which life could thrive, it was received as death. What is a teen to do with that?

She reads *Chain Reaction*, the story of Columbine High School Shooting victim Rachel Scott. Though it is a nearly twenty-year-old school tragedy, it has marked our state of Colorado. Littleton is not so far from us. Rachel's father

---

71. C. S. Lewis, *Weight of Glory* (New York: Harper One, 2001) rep. ed., 46.

includes an essay his daughter wrote about her code of life in which she says, "How do you know that trust, compassion, and beauty will not make this world a better place to be in and this life a better one to live? My codes may seem like a fantasy that can never be reached, but test them for yourself, and see the kind of effect they have in the lives of people around you. You just may start a chain reaction."[72]

Months after the shooting that killed thirteen people, video was released that showed the shooter saying something eerily similar: "We need an [expletive] kick-start—we need to get a chain reaction going here! It's going to be like Doom [the video game] man, after the bombs explode."[73] Two kids, with two different visions. Both desiring to create a chain reaction. Both successful. Eric Harris's "caused death, suffering, mourning, anger, accusations, lawsuits, political debate, and more negative repercussions. Meanwhile, Rachel's chain reaction, which was inspired by her own code of ethics, has created an entirely different set of results."[74]

We create life or death in our words and actions. Though few end in real death, many cause wounds. May we be women who are a salve to the world because we exude life.

It is a season of exciting independent films hitting Redbox and we settle in for a long weekend of Kleenex and popcorn. *Skateistan* speaks to my Afghan-loving heart and I can't wait to show Ella the power of creative engagement with kids to completely alter the trajectory of their lives. It is the story of how a few expats use skateboards to transform the children in Makroyan, a suburb of Kabul. We are amazed at the

72. Darrel Scott, *Chain Reaction* (Nashville, TN: Thomas Nelson, 2001), 56.
73. Ibid., 60.
74. Ibid., 60.

increased confidence in the kids, not to mention the joy and healthy relational involvement it brings. Skateboards brought beauty to Kabul.

In another part of the world, life and beauty entered the slums of Kolkata through the compassion of an Albanian nun. *The Letters* is the story of Mother Teresa's dedication to the poor and her radical belief that they should be cared for with dignity, human touch, and God's love. This humble woman created life and beauty among a people and culture not her own for over sixty years.

By the time we watch *Many Beautiful Things*, about the life of Lilias Trotter, I've just about used up all teen patience with me and indie films. Global sisters are one thing. Historical ones are another. Thankfully, Ella so loves my intentionality, she agrees to one more. Lilias had the potential to become one of the Victorian world's leading artists. Mentored (and even wooed) by famous art critic John Ruskin, she could not resist the seemingly crazy call of God to go to Algeria and serve women and children. Though Ruskin said her work could be immortal, Lilias chose to create art out of an obscure life among Algeria's poor. Lilias's decision feels familiar. Her 99 percent? It may have been good for her to become a well-known female artist, but it was not the job she felt designed to do. The art she felt created to offer was in a foreign land among foreign women.

Esther's Story

I find the story of Esther to be a bit dicey. I've visited harems after all, seen the latticed screen through which women could glimpse state visits and exciting activity of the sultan. History tells us that in times of war, beautiful virgins were spared the sword and made concubines while many men were castrated and turned into guardians of the harem. When we read of Esther enduring twelve months of beauty treatments before being summoned for one night with the king, let us not miss the nuance: she has one opportunity to dazzle this man in bed or risk a lifetime among hundreds of other concubines, trapped behind palace walls.

Esther's rise to fame comes five years after being chosen as queen, when she uses her position of influence over the king to save her people. In a masterful weave of seduction and appetite, she creates a sensual dinner, not once, but twice, to win the king's favor. Again, we would be naive to think the meal ended with food and wine. Esther delighted the king's every sense, bringing to bear her beauty and creativity in exchange for Jewish life. We cannot know if there was any love exchanged in their marriage. We cannot know Esther's feelings surrounding the impossible position she faced in the palace. I dare say, we can barely guess the sexual climate and normative behavior of men and women in ancient Susa. What we can surmise is that Esther "created beauty and glory out of the ashes of the fall." Perhaps her uncle Mordecai's famous charge "for such a time as this" echoed in her soul, as it does in so many of our souls today.

Ella's Experience

We live mere miles from a state university, which hosted its first annual girls STEM (science, technology, engineering, and math) day. Lately, this is the direction Ella's creativity is pointed. Perhaps her favorite gift ever is the old laptop we gave her to take apart. When we send her to STEM day, she knows little of engineering. Girls have to see other women doing something to imagine themselves in their shoes. When she comes home she is dreaming. A new tech club starts at school with the science teacher and she joins. Lately, she thinks she'll become a biochemical engineer. I have no idea what this means except she imagines she might build things to help people. She has a vision to create life and beauty out of science.

Where I lack a framework for science, I have one for words. I take my daughters to a Christian writer's conference with a kids' track. Again, I want them exposed to women creating life and beauty out of their passion, out of what they were designed to offer to the world as a reflection of God's glory. They hear from Kayla Woodhouse, a young woman bearing two titles: one of a few people in the world with a nerve condition in which she does not sweat or feel pain, and the youngest author to have a full-length novel published with a royalty-paying publisher. In spite of the former, Kayla has excelled as an author and speaker, inspiring audiences to live lives set apart for Jesus. My girls are inspired to mine for the truths in their own experiences and shape them into words that bring life.

I myself am at a writers' conference the weekend my youth photojournalism project debuts at a human rights film festival. I have spent months working with six high school students to interview and photograph ten community leaders engaged in anti–human trafficking work. Their work is featured at the festival and my professor friend is moderating one of the trafficking films. I send my husband with Ella to view the exhibit, watch the film, and listen to my friend lead a room full of people. I work hard to create space for justice, to empower teenagers, and to expose good work being done by good people in our town. So does my friend. Ella is moved by everyone's dedication to raise awareness of this human rights crisis.

I wonder, where are you exuding life? Where are the

places in which your daughter can best sneak a look at your life outpour? Are you a small-business owner? Pushing into growth, offering your first webinar, training your first consultant? Are you discipling a new friend? Hosting your third block party? Spending your time pouring into suburban moms and inviting them to church? What is the art you feel designed to offer? Perhaps you've yet to identify it. Perhaps you still need to name your 99 percent. I imagine if you were to take inventory of your life, you would see all the clues right there, staring at you for so long. You were made to create life and beauty. Find it, name it, and then invite your daughter to discover her own 99 percent.

> *Lord of the 99 percent, God of art and creativity, lead this mother and daughter to discover the beautiful, unique ways You designed them to bring forth life and beauty into this world.*

Questions for you:

1. How do you respond when you hear the word *art*? Creative? Are you able to embrace the art you were designed to make?

2. Can you name a place where you bring forth life and beauty?

3. As you consider your daughter, where is she creating life and beauty out of the ordinary? How can you encourage her in that direction?

4. What is invisible right now that you need to make visible? How can you lift it up and declare it holy? Declare it *gift*?

Books for Her to Read	Books I'm Reading	Scripture	Films to Watch	Activities	Gift
Chain Reaction by Darrell Scott	*A Million Little Ways* by Emily P. Freeman	2 Corinthians 2:15	*Skateistan: Four Wheels and a Board in Kabul*	Studio with Sandy	Get one of her games printed
		Esther	*The Letters: The Untold Story of Mother Teresa*	STEM day at CSU	
			Many Beautiful Things	Writers' conference kids' track	
			The Diary of Anne Frank	Human rights film festival with Dad	

Books for Her to Read	Books I'm Reading	Scripture	Films to Watch	Activities	Gift

Part 3

A LIFE BECOMING

A LIFE BECOMING

11

Where Are You Going?

We are running out of time when we realize we are in the wrong place. They will close in a few minutes and our trip will switch to plan B before it even begins. This feels intolerable and so hoisting our backpacks to jog through Dam Square, at rush hour, seems like the only logical thing to do. We must get to the bike rental before closing. This is how it comes to be that a sixty-eight-year-old, forty-two-year-old, and a thirteen-year-old American are found dodging people, cars, and bikes on foot, just moments before they repeat the same maneuvering on wheels. This is how Ella's *Becoming* legacy trip begins, the culmination of her yearlong rites of passage.

We have come to the Netherlands for adventure: to bike a hundred-plus miles in search of strong female examples of our five scaffolding categories and to bless Ella as she passes the test and enters the sisterhood of women. My mom has joined and is probably in the best shape of all of us. We have studied the bike maps, joined a bike community to stay with hosts along the way, and learned a bit about some of the Dutch women we hope to encounter. It is the flattest country in the world with more bikes than humans. We got this! How hard can it be?

We make it to the shop before closing, but not before

doubting the whole plan. We witness the madness of Amsterdam on bikes and wonder if we'll even get out of the center to our hostess's house. The owner starts doling out supplies: a repair kit, even though we've never had a flat. Extra bungee cords, even though you shouldn't need them for your bags. Locks upon locks and make sure you use this key before this key. All of this will become pertinent, but right now? Now we are fixated on the flow of traffic and how to jump into the stream.

The triumph of our first stoplight warrants an elated high-five. We are together, intact, bags still attached. However, it is only this first stroke of luck we can celebrate as the next light sends Ella into a stream going in a different direction, my mom's bag topples to the street, and I wobble on my bike made for giant Dutch people. Thousands upon thousands of pedestrians, cyclists, and motorists crisscross the lanes we share. It is utter madness, terrifying. Two hours later we finally traverse two miles and arrive at Daphne's home, our first hostess, trembling.

Despite rush hour insanity the night before, the next day we miraculously make it to the train station, to the bike car, on and off again without incident. We are biking from Utrecht to Gouda, with stops at a castle, windmill, and a witches weighing station. Our bike map looks straightforward enough. To see the statue of Trijn van Leemput, who led a group of Dutch women to storm the ruling Spanish castle in 1577, we head for the city center. After wandering and circling, we pop into a tourist office to confirm she exists and not only learn that they've never heard of this great heroine, but that our bike map is outdated: the whole country has changed its trail numbering system. "Do not worry," they say. "It is easier now," they say. "Have this map," they say.

The first path winds out of town to a fork in the road and there is no sign. No number. We are lost within minutes and spend the better part of the day lost. It takes hours to get out of this town. We ask countless Dutch people for help until one woman has us follow her all the way to the castle. She offers for us to crash at her place and admits that numbering the bike paths is the last thing Utrecht will do in its city expansion planning. At some point, I lose all sensation in my butt. On this, the first day, I have not yet discovered the bike path app. I have not yet learned to take pictures of the maps we encounter in random places along the way. I have not yet embraced the beauty of the metaphor. Plan B has devolved into plan C, which has forced me to devise plan D.

But the people are stunning. Remarkably helpful. And soon, we are not surprised. In every town we see statues of women, heroines from the sixteenth century who stood up to Spain or led her people to resist tyranny (fighting for what they believe in). We stay with noble women who show us generous hospitality (creating life and beauty out of what they have). We spy remnants of the female Dutch resistance in Anne Frank's attic, Corrie ten Boom's hiding place, and the Begijnhof (women humbly sacrificing without losing their voice). We have lunch with a justice seeker at Not for Sale's training-restaurant for men and women coming out of sex trafficking. It is apparent we are among a great and glorious sisterhood, past and present.

As it turns out, biking in the Netherlands is an awful lot like life. Plan as you might, there will be detours, poor signage, and lots of confusion along the way. Keep your eyes open for kindness, because it is plentiful, and those folks will serve as guides, helpmates on the journey. It is tiring and sometimes, you just stop feeling certain body parts. Doing it with people you love is key and makes it worth it, but making sure everyone has adequate equipment is quite helpful. Sometimes, the stench of sheep goes on for miles, reminding you that this is not your home, but a fallen world, and making your eyes sting because it's just that toxic. And the one nagging question you'll ask yourself each day is, *Where the heck am I going?*

We have framed the year of *Becoming* around God's questions to Hagar: Where have you come from and where are you going? You rooted your daughter in her family narrative, spent a year building a scaffolding of womanhood, and are now inviting her to the company of women by posing the question, *Where are you going?*

We return to the well and a frightened, stubborn maidservant carrying her master's baby. The angel of the Lord asks Hagar his questions and don't you wonder, *Where was she going?* The desert road to Shur is on the way back to Egypt. Was she headed to perceived familiarity? Comfort? Maybe just a bigger city where she could hide in anonymity. Dare we say she was headed away from her calling, from the place and people out of which her blessing would emerge? For when God speaks, he promises her descendants too numerous to count, just like he promised Abram. "Where are you going Hagar?" for your calling is *that way. Go back and step into who God designed you to be.*

The year of *Becoming* is drawing to an end, but the journey of answering this question is just beginning. I do not expect many thirteen-year-old girls to know the answer, but I long for them to know it's a question to wrestle with, truly a process of discovery. If you've done your job well, you've cast a vision of who God has designed her to be. You've called her to an altogether bigger story. You've lifted her eyes above the teen obsession with bodies, boys, and besties and inspired her to more. Finding the answers to the "more" is what starts after the *Becoming* year.

Crafting the Legacy Event

Elements of a Test

As you design your legacy event, I pray it will be a unique and beautiful reflection of your daughter and your relationship with her. It may be a trip or a special day in your hometown. It may involve an entire group of moms and daughters, or you and your spouse, or just you and your daughter. There is no one way to conclude the *Becoming* year. The important thing is that you bring it to a close with these three elements present: a challenge or test of some sort, a culmination of the scaffolding, and a blessing and invitation to womanhood. I call it a legacy event because it will leave a lasting, life-altering memory in your daughter's life and impact future generations.

1. *Challenge*

The Bible is replete with physical and mental challenges its characters must endure to become more fully themselves in all their glory: Abraham must hike the mountain with Isaac, build an altar, and hope for a ram. Jacob must wrestle with the angel of the Lord. Joseph must endure prison. Ruth must harvest on the edge of the fields and wait to be noticed by Boaz. Esther must receive twelve months of beauty treatments and win the favor of the king. David must survive Saul. Mary must carry the scorn and shame that comes with carrying the Savior. Jesus endures forty days of temptation. Saul loses his sight in order to see Jesus.

I believe there is something intrinsic in us all to embrace, endure, and conquer challenges. Several reality TV shows come to mind: *In the Wild* with Bear Grills, *Survivor, The*

Amazing Race, Ninja Warrior, The Voice, America's Got Talent. Do not all of these have an element of risk? A testing of grit, determination, and ability? Don't we crave such shows? I don't know about your children, but mine are not watching for mere entertainment, but rather comparison. They are asking the questions: *Could I? Would I? Will I?*

As you consider your daughter, what kind of challenge is appropriate? What will push her a little, yet be within her skill set? What will feel like a test, yet still be fun? What will be a call to rise to the challenge, yet have a certainty of completion? My two girls are unique, different from each other. For Ella, it was physical (a hundred miles on a bike!) but for my youngest daughter, I'm brainstorming other things more appropriate for her. The important thing is that when our daughters look to their reservoir of character and conviction, will they find what it takes to meet the challenge?

2. Cumulative

Was she paying attention? You've spent a year building a scaffolding of womanhood, naming key categories and soaking in them through a variety of senses. What did she learn? When Jesus was in the wilderness for forty days, he responded to each temptation with Scripture. As it applies to our kids, we've created the framework throughout the year and now when given the opportunity to hang meaning upon it, can they do it? When Jesus was enticed with specific temptations, He could resist because He knew His Father's will so clearly. When your daughter is offered a specific scenario, can she enter in fully, understanding clearly what she should do?

How will you create your legacy event? For our son, the men on the trail read realistic situations that required one of the aspects of manhood he had learned. Aidan had to explain which one fit best and why in order to get the brick and move on. Below, you'll read about what I did for Ella. For both rites of passage, we interweaved the physical challenge with the cumulative knowledge. My youngest is quite artistic and also into spy stuff. I'm starting to think about how to create an event that weaves great artistic masters and their work with elements of mystery. I'm wondering about the role of these new escape rooms that are gaining popularity. Here's the point: our daughters are unique and each test should reflect this. There is no right or wrong here. Remember, we've created a paradigm of being, not a prescription for living.

3. Blessing and Inviting

This is what it has all been for: blessing your daughter's voice as it reflects the glory of God, and inviting her to leave childhood behind and begin the journey of womanhood. She needs to know the rites of passage is done. She needs to know she passed. She needs to be welcomed to the company of women. If we fail to do this for our daughters, she will wonder for years, *Am I a woman?*

The Bible is full of blessings. In fact, before and after almost every challenge, God bestows a blessing. The Father blesses the Son at the Jordan River just before he begins his public ministry. Jesus asks John to baptize him and when he comes out of the water, the Spirit descends and a voice is heard: "This is my Son, chosen and marked by my love, delight of my life."[75] A new season has begun and the invitation is clear. God the Father names his Son, not only as chosen, but as His delight. What will you name your daughter?

---

75. Matthew 3:17 (MSG).

Play the role of exegete and name what you see in her. Name how she exhibits the categories you've discussed. Speak them into existence in her life. I encourage you to write it down so that she can go back and remind herself, so that she never forgets who she is. And finally, invite her to join you in the process of becoming. Tell her it has just begun, but that she is now a part of the sisterhood, part of the legacy of women, past, present, and future.

Grandma's Reflections

Joining my daughter and granddaughter in the Becoming *year was significant for me. In a small way, we journeyed together, with me growing as much as my granddaughter! As a result, I've reflected on my own life, maybe deeply for the first time! What is my story?*

Coming from a very traditional home, I remember my mother always present, devoted to my well-being, and providing the essentials. I think I turned out okay. But I realized I missed intentional development of me. I was told I could do anything I wanted to do in life, but what did that mean and how could I? There was no discussion about women in history, in the Bible, in my own family, and the qualities that made them strong women of faith. I didn't realize there was any connection between them and me. Would my life had been different if my mom had intentionally planned these discussions about the qualities that made women strong?

Ella's journey has just begun, but she already knows what it will take as she joins a greater company of women. I have been on my journey for quite a long time, and am continuing to discover God's plan for me. I am anxious to focus on the rest of my story, as I realize the process of Becoming *never ends.*

What Did I Do?

I chose a bike trip in the Netherlands for a number of reasons. Ella needed a physical challenge because that's the kind of person she is and my mom and I enjoy biking far more than hiking. I had a hunch that a land that produced Corrie ten Boom and Anne Frank had many other stories of strong women. And I knew there was amazing work happening in the red-light district where we could experience our sisters being both exploited and responding to exploitation with strength and resolve. On all counts, I was right (thank You, Jesus).

The actual test needed to unfold throughout our trip and I couldn't plan exactly what stories of women we would encounter when. So, going on her love for scavenger hunts and riddles, I found a brass cryptex (think *Da Vinci Code*) that unlocked with a five-letter word. I programmed in *voice* and snuck two small gifts inside. On day one of our trip, we grabbed breakfast in a café and I issued the challenge: she would carry around the cryptex until she could unlock it. Each time she saw an example of a woman (past or present) exhibiting one of the five categories of our scaffolding, she would elaborate how and then receive a note written by one of the women who participated in *Becoming*. At the bottom of their message to her would be an alphabet letter for the puzzle. It was such fun—mysterious and challenging all at once! I loved being able to include the women who helped with our year and actually have my mom with us the whole time.

Thankfully, discovering examples of women was not as difficult as finding the numbered bike paths. From statues to museums to our very hostesses, identifying the categories of our scaffolding was easy! Indeed, throughout time and throughout the globe, women lead, women love, women fight, women sacrifice, and women create. They do so because God has created us in His image.

On our last night in Amsterdam, Ella received her final letter and opened the cryptex. Inside I had placed two small gifts. The first, the pendant Arwen wears in *The Fellowship of the Ring*, a symbol of her immortality. She sacrificed it out of love for Aragorn. But I gave it to Ella as a symbol of the quiet, oft invisible strength she'll be called to exhibit in life. As she finds and uses her voice, it does not *have* to be a loud, visible display of power. There is a silent, but powerful display of strength in Arwen's sacrifice. The second gift, a picture of the small dagger waiting for her at home. This is a symbol of taking up the fight against those who would seek to diminish or destroy her voice, including herself. There will be times in life when she will wield this symbolic dagger to protect her glory: may she never believe she is too much or not enough!

She had three more letters to read: from her dad, my mom, and me. They served to be the final blessing and invitation. As my husband wrote,

Ella, you lead, you fight, you sacrifice, you love, you create. You are a true woman. Now at the end of your *Becoming* year, you embark on a new adventure. The world awaits, and so desperately needs a true woman like you to bring the fullness of her voice, beauty, and femininity to alter the course of history.

Where there is brokenness, healing. Where there is despair, hope. Where there is hate, love. Where there is aimlessness and confusion, leadership. Where there is void, life. Where there is abuse and exploitation, protection and freedom. There is no power equal to a true woman's voice. There will be no power equal to yours.

Dear Ella,

If all has gone according to plan, we've had an amazing week of testing our strength and testing your knowledge of what it means to be created in God's image as a woman. The question has been, do you have what it takes? The biking was merely a metaphor, for on this journey of becoming, the ultimate question that needs to be answered is, "Where are you going?"

We answered the question, "Where have you come from?" in Turkey: you've come from a rich and storied heritage of women who have chosen to follow the small still voice of God, who are beautiful in their strength and weakness. You were born during a season of intense love and stress and struggle. Is it any wonder you are strong and adventuresome? We rooted you in the Bruno story by going back to Turkey.

We spent the year exploring ways in which women best reflect God's glory: they lead, they love, they fight, they sacrifice, and they create. And while you have properly identified those categories this week, let me tell you how I see you already embodying them in your life:

Ella, you lead. You lead with the skills you have to benefit others. I saw this when you herded the little kids in the play and taught them their dances. I saw this when you spoke up for the girl in art who was not being treated well.

Ella, you love. You love because God first loved you. When you realized that loving your friends well meant not making it about you, but modeling yourself after Jesus (who laid down his life for his friends), I knew you got it. You show love every time you hand a homeless person one of your bags.

Ella, you fight. When you weep for Talia, you are fighting for her soul. When you championed the cause of human trafficking in your class, you brought education to students in a way that may save someone someday.

Ella, you sacrifice. It was no small thing to delay changing your own room or getting new things for yourself in order to bring about a transformation to your sister's room. This was huge.

Ella, you create. You bring life and beauty to your friendships every time your loyalty wins, every time you are kind, every time you refrain from gossip, every time you embrace the lonely. You create beauty in all that you breathe life into: duct tape creations, writing, singing, song-writing, game making, decorating, designing, engineering.

And now this brings us to God's second question to Hagar: "Where are you going?" Every woman comes to a moment of discovering her place in God's story. What story is He writing for you? What passion will you pursue as you come alongside Him to bring His kingdom to earth as it is in heaven? What about Jesus' heart breaks your heart? When you find the answers to these questions, you will know where you are going. It may not be now, but my goal in this whole year was to cast a vision for who you are becoming and to what I'm inviting you.

I am inviting you to bring it. Bring all of you to this world right now. Don't wait until you're twenty or thirty or forty. The world needs you right now. God wants to use you right now. Enter His story. Find the answer to where you are going. Ella, you are a voice becoming. Use it.

Welcome to womanhood.

Every woman comes to a moment of discovering her place in God's story. What story is He writing for you? What passion will you pursue as you come alongside Him to bring His kingdom to earth as it is in heaven? What about Jesus' heart breaks your heart? When you find the answers to these questions, you will know indeed where you are going.

Chart for Crafting Your Legacy Event

Challenge: Does She Have What It Takes?	Cumulative: Was She Listening?	Blessing and Inviting: Welcome to Womanhood	Where?	With Whom?	Details

12

A Voice Becoming:
A Story Unfolding

Ten days after our bike trip, we were in the ER.

Summer had begun in glory and nothing but goodness stretched before us. Our sixteen-year-old drove himself to his first job. Our ten-year-old walked to the pool alone. And Ella had her first babysitting gig, watching two boys who simply adored her. My husband and I were counting down the days until everyone went to camp and we would have a week to ourselves in the mountains. The hope-filled plans were abundant.

On the last day of the first week of summer, Ella played wildly with the boys on their trampoline, jumped beneath the spray of water from the hose hanging above the net, and landed in all the wrong ways. Ten hours later, after morphine, CAT scans, and surgery, she emerged from anesthesia with four pins and a metal plate in her leg. Summer abruptly ended.

After days of alternately eating chips and chocolate, cleaning out closets and files like a madwoman, and weeping into my pillow, I realized I was the only one reacting this way. Ella was either in shock, denial, or far more mature than me. Her attitude was serene. Maybe even godly. As in, the peace of God seemed to have descended upon her. She woke through the night in pain. Narcotics had wreaked havoc on her digestive system. She could not move, nor would be allowed to put weight on her leg for twelve weeks! Her job was over. Camp was out. Hiking the annual fourteener was out. And our family trip to Chicago would require a wheelchair. And yet.

Ella was devoid of anger or pity. While some kids (perhaps even her siblings!) might hold the family in a state of bitter "woe is me" comparison, Ella created life and beauty out of her circumstances. Her words were kind instead of caustic. Her attitude was grateful instead of resentful. I was amazed.

Brené Brown tells the story of asking the creator of *Grey's Anatomy* and *Scandal* about the role of struggle in storytelling. She responded to Brené, "I don't even know who a character is until I've seen how they handle adversity. Onscreen and off-screen, that's how you know who someone is."[76]

In a divine act, I believe God gave us the opportunity to catch a glimpse of who Ella is becoming. Throughout our intentional rites of passage year, I certainly noticed moments of clarity and application, when she surprised even herself by living out the theme we were discussing. But after a year of talking, reading, watching, and experiencing all the things we did, how would I really know what it had amounted to?

As the story of our daughters' lives unfold, as they begin the journey of becoming women, struggles will reveal what they are really made of. Adversity will test their grit.

I vividly remember my first test. After trusting Jesus after talking with Randy Matthews at a ski retreat my freshman year, I continued to slowly grow in my faith. Most of the kids

76. Brené Brown, *Rising Strong: The Reckoning. The Rumble. The Revolution* (New York: Spiegel & Grau, 2016), 42.

around me went to Young Life and youth group and generally stayed out of trouble. At least, until they could drive. As soon as the freedom of the car came into play, deception followed. By my junior year, weekend parties bounced around parent-free houses and were full of alcohol, pot, and closed doors. I was slowly losing my friends as I became designated driver and vomit cleaner.

On top of this, my dad's mom moved in with us, with a new muscle disease and a steroid prescription that made her crazy. And my mom's dad was spending his last days on a sugar-water-morphine drip six hours north. We spent weekdays caring for one grandparent and weekends driving to see another.

Ironically, it was not the friend crisis or the night on the floor in the baby-blue bathroom, sobbing after my grandfather's last breath, but a math class that brought me to my knees—the final test. In the midst of all this, I could not keep up with precalculus. Every day Ms. Hoza would begin class with, "Comments, questions, drop slips?" until one day, I said yes. It was my first encounter with failure, the first time I admitted weakness and imperfection.

And it drove me to Jesus. I learned to pray and rely on someone other than myself. I needed Him heavily and found Him in the simple answers given to those in the early days of faith: my grandfather died, ending the painful, drawn-out march to death; my grandmother moved out, restoring unity in my parents' marriage; I began to make new friends, giving me a social outlet besides the pot-infused brownie gatherings; a new math class introduced me to a whole new group of kids from various economic, social, and racial backgrounds that planted a seed of curiosity in me. I would choose Jesus in the face of all this adversity and in doing so, become more of myself.

How has struggle helped to write your story of *Becom-*

ing? Who is the character you have become? And what of your daughter? While I would not wish adversity upon anyone, life is life, is it not? It's not if, but when, struggle will come. And when the "when" arrives, who is she? Pay attention, for she may have much to teach you.

Ella started eighth grade in a cast. Translation: She entered the building alone each day, the only one allowed to take the elevator to the third floor; she lagged behind the crowd at passing periods and on the way from lunch to recess; she sat with the teacher during PE and heard snippets of gossip as groups cycled past jogging the mile. All the ingredients for an emotional start, especially for a relationally wired, sensitive girl. Especially since every other new school year since third grade had started off with tears and breakdowns.

And yet. Something was different. After a few afternoons of tears, I noticed an abrupt shift. The bag of bricks she had been carrying around (the perceived negative looks, comments, and actions) dropped. She started to treat them as Post-it notes, little things that stuck to her, but floated away and all the more quickly if she brushed them off. I saw a strength of self, a grounding of her soul. She was solid.

A few weeks into the school year, a group of moms in the same life stage gathered around a fire pit for cocktails and conversation. Sure enough, several middle-school daughters were starting the year off similarly. I ached for the moms because it brings up all of our own memories from adolescence and junior high. It seems unfair to have to relive those days through our children!

Unsure of whether Ella's shift was due to her age, the transition to eighth grade, or perhaps my intentionality with her the previous year, I shared that this was the first fall since third grade that I was not picking up emotional pieces each night. I admitted it was a welcomed relief and I felt the other mothers' pain, deeply. A friend with older girls affirmed my hunch though. She agreed it was probably more about my intentionality than a natural by-product of age. She had seen something similar in her own daughter.

Could it be that I was already seeing the antidote to her obsession with besties? Could it be God was affirming this rites of passage year just as I needed to start writing about it? A whisper, *Take heart*, this was not a waste of time? So I could turn to fellow moms and say, with all my heart and soul, this is so, so worth it?

Ella's Reflections

Yes, it is true. My mom is out to wreck me. And she's doing a pretty good job at it too. She uses the struggles of the world to break my heart. She uses those shattered pieces in my soul to motivate me. To inspire me. To encourage me to take a stand and use my voice to change the world around me. The outcome of my Becoming year is such vast growth, sometimes I don't recognize myself. Why am I not holding a grudge? How can I speak so freely about God without being embarrassed? How do I know so much about the world? I know why. This year changed me.

In school, my peers are so focused on how they look, their friendships, and the immature boys that roam the halls without a care in the world that they don't think about who they are and who they are to become. They preoccupy their minds with silly crushes (which, honestly, I sometimes have too) and how they look that day. Sometimes they can't focus on schoolwork because their hair is a little poofy.

Here is where I feel different. My mom has given me something else to live for and strive for beyond middle-school drama and immature guys. She's given me a knowledge and open-mindedness for the world that I never saw before. She used those heartbreaking stories to form passion in me. Passion I used to lack. Passion that I will draw from to do some good in the world. My mom set out to wreck me, but only so that I could offer something grand.

Recently I chatted with a mom whose girls are my girls' ages. She is tired. Frustrated. Feels defeated by screens, apps, and social media. She and her oldest argue a lot. They miss each other on multiple heart levels. Like many moms I've talked with, she tried the book, or went to that mother-daughter event at church, or already did the thing with her dad and the whole Sunday school. While those were special events, she and her daughter are still where they are. And she has given up. Teens will be teens. The rites of passage she has bought into? The teenage years parallel the toddler years: hold your breath and bear it, it's a season.

Oh, moms. No. No! Don't believe it. Don't hold your breath and give up. Don't give in! It doesn't have to be that way. Listen to me: The relentless pursuit of your daughter's heart will yield fruit of great magnitude. Download the Piano Guys' "Fight Song"–"Amazing Grace" mash-up and take heart. There is more than a season of attitude, more than a season of delayed responsibility, more than an obsession with bodies, boys, and besties that awaits our teenage daughters. But it will require *you* to have eyes to see. It will require *you* to cast a vision.

Our girls were designed for so much more than running ragged between sports and after-school activities. They were designed for deeper relationships than selfies and Snapchat stories. They have the intelligence and passion to do far more than decorate for homecoming. Is it wrong to be involved in these things? No, of course not. But this is not what they were designed for! This is not the pinnacle of the teen years! This is not the measure of their self-worth! And this is not what I want their eyes to land on, obsess over. God has fashioned in them, as his children, a unique purpose that will unfold in a unique story. He has created them to bring about his kingdom on earth as it is in heaven. He has given them a voice and it is powerful, needed, valued. *Malala! Rifqa! Katie Davis!* Might it be used in sports? Yes! Might it be used in student leadership? Yes! But let us align their eyes to the bigger story being told: a loving and gracious God walks among us.

Let me ask a tough question: Where are *your* eyes cast?

The story starts with you. I said that some chapters back. The process of *Becoming* is as much for the mother as it is for the daughter. So let me ask it again. Where are you in your story?

My fun-loving, peacekeeping, modest mother experienced redemption in the ironic timing of my absence when "it happened" for Ella. But it didn't stop there. Through her involvement in the henna night, and her presence for our school-ditching movie date *He Named Me Malala*, and our final epic journey in the Netherlands, she was altogether caught up in her own process of *Becoming*. At age sixty-eight. Her reflection points to the beauty of a life in the making, a life of *Becoming*, a journey of womanhood that never ends. Where are you in *your* journey?

Here's where I hope to be in mine: I want to be a hope-pusher, a darkness-disrupter, a justice-warrior, a grace-clinger. As I lead, love, fight, sacrifice, and create, I want to bring the fullness of who I am to the kingdom of God. Right now, it looks like leading an anti–human trafficking organization, raising three kids, loving my husband well, and writing as an overflow of my 99 percent. I refuse to wear the mantle of shame or feel too much and not enough. I will embrace my weakness and strength, and allow them to be friends. I will offer my voice to the world, cloaked in power and grace. I will cast my eyes above and embrace the process of *Becoming*.

How can I conclude when the story is far from over? Ella deserves the space to fail and I have to resist putting her on a pedestal. You have to resist putting *us* on a pedestal. I have endeavored to share our story in hopes of inspiring you to wreck your daughter too. Wreck her for that which wrecks Jesus' heart. Cast a vision of who she is becoming, who she is joining in the story unfolding.

What do you say? Will you join me?

Acknowledgments

Bringing a book into the world is simultaneously a lonely and crowded endeavor. Alone with my words, yet present to the myriad voices who shape and inform nearly every sentence, I find it to be a peculiar experience. Even more bizarre is how seldom these voices know they are in my head. To the few whom I can thank, would you know how beautiful your voice is to me.

Mom, Casey, Gissela, Jess, Jenni, Sandy—for joining in the journey and going places that may have felt uncomfortable, for helping me raise my daughter and loving both of us as you do, thank you.

Greg and Jess—for doing life with us and being the aunt and uncle in proximity that our kids have needed, thank you.

Eddy and Sandy—your friendship, words, and wisdom were my muse. Thank you.

Jenni—for processing, and crying, with me along the way. Thank you.

Mara and Mindy—for not only teaching me about purity, but introducing me to Jesus. In so many ways, my story starts with you both. Thank you.

Tawny and DC Jacobson Agency—your belief in me and this project from the beginning was a game changer. I'm so thrilled to have you in this journey.

Keren and HBG team—for championing my voice to a new generation of women in such an honoring and supportive way, thank you.

Redbud Writer's Guild—everything I know about the business and discipline and calling of writing I know from these women. They have made me a writer. For the unique assistance along the way—Margot, Aleah, Catherine, and Dorothy, thank you.

For the women of Turkey—Alev, Esra, Zeynep, Kris, Sara, Bethany, and Shelley—who walked with me in strength and would have welcomed weakness had I let you. Thank you for making those years as dear as they were.

Dan Allender—thank you for having such a profound impact on our lives and understanding of story and for the hair story, which never gets old.

The Piano Guys—my soundtrack, my anthem, thank you.

Mom—thank you for letting your story be told in the midst of mine and Ella's. Modesty aside, you are and always have been an incredible role model to me and truly so much of the reason I am who I am today. I am so proud of your own journey and even prouder to be your daughter. And thank you, Dad, for your characteristic support, as always!

Aidan and Sophie—'tis no easy thing to have one sibling enjoy more attention for a time, but your grace and generosity did not go unnoticed or unappreciated. May you see the benefit in your relationships for years to come! I am so proud of you both!

Chris—I can't imagine a life without you by my side. I am so proud and thankful to be your wife, best friend, business partner, fellow dreamer, and coparent. For all that life has brought, and all that is yet to come, I will forever praise God for you, and that you declared, "I want to date you and call it dating."

Ella—what courage to let your story unfold in public. By agreeing to live life out loud with me through this process, think of the moms and daughters you might impact! I began with hope and prayers, but to see who you are becoming has far exceeded what I could have asked or imagined. I can think of no greater gift than to allow me to wreck you so that I might invite you to the story God is telling through you and through your sisters around the world. What a blessing that the journey continues.

Appendix A

Bodies and Bras, Besties and Boys

Here's the thing, dear moms. There is so much to teach our girls. So much. Too much. Are you as overwhelmed as I am? Even as I was preparing for an entire yearlong process of *Becoming*, I knew there were some timely and important categories we needed to address with our daughter. Issues preteens and young teens face that we have to dive right into with them. We can create an elaborate scaffolding of womanhood, but if we miss being intentional about the things she thinks about and struggles with every day, we have failed.

The four categories in this chapter stem from daily conversations that brewed in her eleventh-to-twelfth year. Your daughter may be wrestling with different issues, though I would venture to guess these are ubiquitous among adolescent girls. These were topics we discussed leading up to the launch of *Becoming*, giving her a good foundation for our intentionality. I'm merely skimming over these because, though they are valuable, you can find more thorough coverage in other books and I feel they are of secondary importance to a rites of passage year.

On Bodies

The day I taught Ella to shave, I learned the few elements required to communicate love and intention: my time and attention. It was simple and not well planned. We were headed into shorts season and she was joining the swim team. For months, she had been asking about shaving and complaining about her hairy legs. I purchased a cute razor, splurged on shaving cream and put them in a little gift bag. The rest of the family was gone and I told Ella to put on her swimsuit and meet me in my bathroom.

She entered confused by the candles and music and warm running water, just about as cheesy as I'm capable of getting. All in all, we spent a grand total of fifteen minutes learning how to shave, but she was enthralled by the feel of her skin and how grown-up she felt. I realized I had primed her for some deeper discussion by pouring into her, giving my full love and attention to only her.

Time to pounce.

Off and on throughout fifth grade, she had bemoaned the size of her thighs, her height, and other features she disliked. As one of the taller kids in her class, she was never the kid on the top of pyramids or chosen to do cheer throws at recess. Little comments not meant to harm, like "Oh, you're heavy!" reduced her to sobs at home. The irony of course, is that she is incredibly thin and athletic. And yet, as so many girls do, she started struggling with body image at the ripe age of ten! Recently, my fourth-grade daughter burst into tears out of nowhere. She said sometimes she had bad thoughts when she took a shower. After undressing, she would look in the mirror and feel fat and ugly and think horrible things about herself. Though they are both trim and fit, I was amazed at how early on and how core to their image this struggle is!

Beauty and body appreciation was a topic I knew my girls and I would revisit many times. So, after we shaved, I pulled out my laptop and Ella and I sat together on my bathroom floor. She rubbed her legs up and down as we watched the Dove beauty commercials, first the Photoshop one that shows the transformation of a "normal" looking young woman into a model on a billboard; then the artist one in which women describe another woman and themselves to a sketch artist and then see the comparison. At the reveal, the women's descriptions of themselves are consistently less flattering than the stranger's description. Admittedly, I cried. Body image runs deep for most moms, no?

I don't love my body. I strongly dislike shopping, can never buy clothes online, dread swimsuit season and haven't really worn shorts for a decade. But these are feelings I mostly share with God and my journal. Occasionally, I complain to my husband, but he learned years ago that most of these conversations end badly for him. Knowing he will choose silence and tender looks to feeding me the lines I long to hear, but will accuse him of making up, I now refrain from even starting.

But one thing I have internally vowed to never do is complain about my body or discuss how I feel with my daughters. They do not need to know that I wish I could lose twenty pounds. They need me to put on my suit and jump in the pool with them. My trips to the gym are casually mentioned in the context of my day and because we value healthy living and exercise, not because I feel guilty if I don't go. *Diet* is a bad word in our home. I refuse to raise kids who think about their weight and looks as much as I do. And while I can't shield them from other kids, media, and culture icons, I can at the very least shield them from my own issues. I can give them a counter-story.

So even though I had already watched the Dove commercials, there I was again, tears streaming down my face. Ella noticed.

Ella: Mom, what is it?

Me: Aw, Ella. It's just so sad how we view ourselves, you know? I mean, look at that woman and how pretty she is, but look at how she thinks of herself. That drawing is nothing like her, but it's how she feels. What if we saw ourselves the way God sees us?

Ella: Yeah, it's really a big difference.

Me: So, what are the things about yourself that you don't like? How would you describe yourself?

Ella: Well, I think my lips are enormous. Like gross they're so huge! And look at my legs! [as she jiggles her quad muscle]

Me: And I would say your lips are one of your most beautiful features and plenty of women have surgery to make their lips bigger like yours. And your legs, well, those are athlete legs. They aren't toothpicks because you have muscle!

She began to smile even though she wasn't sure she wanted to believe me. Self-perception is hard to change. I should know. Is it even possible? To convince a tween that she has a perfect and lovely body?

I shared Psalm 139: "Body and soul, I am marvelously made! I worship in adoration—what a creation! You know me inside and out, you know every bone in my body; You know exactly how I was made, bit by bit, how I was sculpted from nothing into something." May we know it in the core of our beings, she and I.

On Bras

Truth be known, I am afraid of the lingerie department. Every few years, I decide it is time for some new bras. I wait for sales and head to Kohl's, but I always inevitably freeze, unable to comprehend the hundreds of varieties, completely clueless and incapable of deciding. Why, I must ask, are there so many kinds of bras? So many brands, so many colors, so many sizes, so many styles. And expensive! I wander aimlessly, eyes wide, sticker shock slowing my pace until I start to panic and quickly leave. I end up buying cheap alternatives I don't like from Target and forgetting the experience over the next few years until I repeat the same cycle. Can you picture me in Victoria's Secret?

I have decided something must have gone wrong with me. This was surely my mom's job to instruct me. But my one memory of shopping near this department as a child is of my two-year-old brother loudly calling out, "Mom, what are those?" while pointing to a mannequin's bra-clad breasts. Perhaps, this is why I never learned how to bra shop.

Determined to break this chain of ignorance and fear, I take Ella to the store. We are going to grow up together. We head there after weeks of her complaining that her training bras are too small and after I've already made my first pass through Kohl's. The season had arrived for me too. We are in the section and I'm explaining my fear to her, refusing to make eye contact with other women, trying to look like I know what I'm doing. I show her the numbers and letters and wires. I do know something! But it's obvious that the smallest of options are too large for her. We're in the wrong place.

A salesperson walks by and I start, "Are there teenage..." but trail off. Bless her heart, she finishes my sentence, "Bras. Yes, there are junior bras in the kids' section." Ella and I walk away smiling. We are hopelessly modest; can you imagine us going somewhere to be properly measured? But we are brave, courageous women, headed to pick out BRAS! And when we choose two each and pay the ridiculously high price of eighty-two dollars and head home with our purchases, we are new people. We are proud and empowered and grown-up. Oh, how grown-up! We survived the intimates section, together.

But barely. What universe are we in that padded bras form the bulk of choices in the kids' department? Why do eleven-year-old girls need a chest? Which brings up a whole separate topic of modesty. Oh, what a word! Thankfully, Ella wasn't tempted by cleavage, but we've had our fair share of talks about tank tops and short shorts. Modesty bears mentioning.

And yet I hate the word. It brings up memories of being separated at Christian conferences to talk to girls about modesty and boys about lust. It reminds me of my early days overseas, wearing hideous skirts to divert attention from my Western "looseness," when the attention actually came from being foreign. I could have worn hijab and men still would have stared at my blue eyes and pale skin. Modesty seems to be a relative and highly inflammatory subject. Who is responsible, what are we protecting, and what are we trying to achieve?

I love how Kate Conner, author of *Enough*, handles this topic. She says, "Modesty is about dressing on purpose. It is about being mature enough to reckon with some realities: the reality that men like to look at women; the reality that if a girl displays her breast overtly, men will stare, no matter how great of guys they are; the reality that clothing speaks and that the way we look matters. Modesty is about choosing clothes that communicate what you want the world to know about yourself; it is an integral part of creating your own, truthful image—the very thing all teenage girls are trying so desperately to do."[77] Conner encourages teens to view modesty as a means of power. How you dress is the best way to control how others think of and relate to you. Do you want to be treated like an intelligent soul? Dress like one. Do you want to be respected? Dress like it.

Modesty as a reflection of your internal world removes

77. Kate Conner, *Enough: 10 Things We Should Be Telling Teenage Girls* (Nashville, TN: B&H Publishing, 2014), 13.

the focus from "causing brothers to stumble" or "covering the body only your husband should see" and other lines we've been told. It is about integrity: a full match of inside and out. In this line of thought, do fake-boob bras fall into the integrity category? Probably not.

On Besties

If there is a prayer I repeat like a broken record it is for Ella to have deep, long-lasting friendships. It feels as though the theme of her school years has been relational drama, angst, and suffering. Many a time I have considered alternative schooling options to escape the agony. I have been crying out to God for years to change the narrative and downright screamed for it to stop. One of my prayers went like so:

> God, I need a break!
>
> I need a break from picking up the pieces every afternoon, as day crawls into evening and we are pulling punching bag upstairs to be beaten and to absorb the pain that we are weary of absorbing…
>
> I need a victory because she needs a victory, desperately, and one that lasts longer than an afternoon.
>
> I need her to come home smiling, for real, and not just because in her immediate hunger and relief to be safe in our kitchen, she has forgotten that she's in pain.
>
> I need her to eagerly walk out the door, just one day, instead of having to nudge her to walk the fifty yards to the bus stop and do it all again.
>
> And it is torture to make us relive this, we who were girls and have already suffered our fair share of junior high days and junior high girls and junior high boys and junior high male teachers who shouldn't be and junior high rejection!

How brutal to resurrect those feelings and double the shame, making every rejection our rejection, again and again.

I need a break!

I'm tired of praying for her best. I want her to win. For once, I want it to go as she wants it to go. I want her to come home victorious, not requiring hours of making sense of it and shaping it into something manageable, tolerable.

I want to stop questioning, every single day, if it's time to fight on her behalf or if this challenge is one to mold her. I am done wondering if she's processing it correctly or through skewed emotion.

So today when she comes home from tryouts and when the cast list is posted, I'm just warning You, I don't have much left. Tank is empty. I'm fragile and cracked. Hear me? Thank You for listening, God. Amen.

Honestly, some of her pain triggers too many of my own childhood memories. We moved a lot, changing schools five times before my freshman year in high school. Raising emotional and relational girls has propelled me back to playgrounds and lunchrooms and locker rooms in too many cities. In an instant, I am that girl with the defected used lacrosse stick, desperately wanting to fit in and meet people, but too awkward and clueless to know she bought a broken stick. Sara Hagerty says "there is a beauty in getting to live your story twice"[78] and so lately, I'm embracing the beauty in reliving it all.

78. Sara Hagerty, *Every Bitter Thing Is Sweet: Tasting the Goodness of God in All Things* (Nashville, TN: Zondervan, 2016), 147.

The hardest thing is knowing that I can't just blame bad kids or bad teachers or poor supervision at recess or on the bus. While these factors produce bad situations, and there are certainly some mean-spirited things girls do to one another, I am fully aware that a good chunk of what I hear through the tears are her own misperceptions and fallacies. And exhaustion.

This finally sunk in a few months into sixth grade. It had been a brutal transition to middle school and the increased requirements and responsibilities of life. More teachers. More classes. More homework. More classmates. More of everything. And less sleep. Less space. Less capacity. She was emotionally thin. I should have predicted the collapse was imminent. It happened on a Monday night.

I wondered, as I always do, how much of what she said was true? Had she really been rejected? Was she really the last person everyone chose to sit by in classes? Did she really walk through the day as lonely and invisible as she felt? And how many of my friends were putting their daughters back together again after their fragility cracked that day? Surely this is a common, heart-wrenching reality all girls face.

So, I woke up Tuesday moaning at God again and begging for an answer, which He surprised me with a few minutes later: Ella pulled a hamstring in dramatic form in PE and was wheeled away in a flurry of activity. Doctors, X-rays, and two crutches later, she lay medicated on the couch. Word spread throughout school and by afternoon, parents of friends were texting me because their daughters had texted them, concerned.

When we entered school the next morning, kids swarmed Ella, kindly and inquisitively wondering what had happened. Girls she had described as thoughtless caressed her arm. Girls she felt abandoned by or invisible to offered assistance. Friends she thought had rejected her on Monday rushed to embrace her on Wednesday. And I wondered, All these years had I been addressing the right things? I've been focused on building her relational strength and resiliency. Maybe part of the issue was coming to conclusions too quickly or writing friendships off based on their immature thoughtlessness or passing moods? Perhaps I needed to help her develop grace and forgiveness for others. What does generous friendship look like? Is there such a thing?

We're given a pretty good picture of generous friendship in the famous love passage of 1 Corinthians 13:

> Love never gives up.
> Love cares more for others than for self.
> Love doesn't want what it doesn't have.
> Love doesn't strut,
> Doesn't have a swelled head,
> Doesn't force itself on others,
> Isn't always "me first,"
> Doesn't fly off the handle,
> Doesn't keep score of the sins of others,
> Doesn't revel when others grovel,
> Takes pleasure in the flowering of truth,
> Puts up with anything,
> Trusts God always,
> Always looks for the best,
> Never looks back,
> But keeps going to the end.[79]

Our home has become a virtual love lab as I've been instructing the kids in how to be friends in this way. "Well, I'm sorry he has the cooler games. Love doesn't want what

---

79. 1 Corinthians 13:4–7 (MSG).

it doesn't have." "That's great you received that honor, but because she didn't, maybe keep it on the down low. Love doesn't strut." "Okay, I know she's driving you crazy, but how can you see her the way God sees her today? Love always looks for the best." "Yeah, we've established she lies, but let's not keep talking about it. Love does not keep score of the sins of others."

Loving well is kind of exhausting. But it is the meat of life. Future spouses, children, coworkers, elderly parents, neighbors, and friends all require we learn to love well. If we can practice this art in the context of current friendships, bestie or not, maybe one day my prayers to God won't be so wrought with agony.

On Boys

When our son was twelve we failed him.

We were in a barbecue restaurant when he leaned over and coyly whispered, "A girl likes me." It was a first! When I asked, and received a confirmed yes to mutual "like" I was pleased. How normal. Our son had a crush. We innocently assumed it would wane in weeks and he'd move on to another crush. So, we didn't share our expectations about relationships or lay down any rules. We didn't even have any! We were new to this and just happy he told us.

Months passed and the crush was still a thing. They were meeting up with other friends at the park, texting like crazy, and generally making us feel like we had lost control. But even though we felt uneasy about the relationship, we failed to intervene. Finally, eight months after the barbecue announcement, I discovered a letter from said crush that freaked me out with its intensity. I went straight to his phone and read the texts and nearly collapsed with how far into the future this girl was dreaming. What could we do? We confronted him, told him it was over, and called her mom and explained our feelings. He was twelve and she was talking baby names!

After he stopped being mad at us, we had a great conversation. Eventually, he even thanked us. Perhaps it was because we asked for his forgiveness. We had failed to protect him by not setting up any expectations, boundaries, or sharing thoughts about girls. We were deeply sorry. But we had also learned a lot. And his sisters would benefit.

From that point on, the kids knew that we would discuss "dating" at age sixteen—when they could actually drive to and pay for a date. This future number is one they have rested in, albeit uncomfortably. Ella has felt secure in this as she watches friend after friend start "dating." After all, it's our fault, not hers, she can reason. But it's still a struggle. To have a boyfriend is to be somebody. To be like everyone else. To be deemed normal, if not cool. She wants a boy to like her for that reason alone. But she has seen the silly immaturities of middle school "love" and is embarrassed on their behalf. She can easily recognize how ill prepared they are for fleeting emotions, jealous Instagram posts, and awkward dances. Knowing the dating conversation will start later gives her a safe zone of reality from which to watch and learn. She knows she is not ready. Crushes? Of course! Relationships? Not now.

I agonize over the balance of keeping her innocent and preparing her for what she needs to know when I think she needs to know it. A teacher took a vote on what the class wanted to read and I had to email him an explanation of why I deem one teen fiction series age appropriate, but another series in the same genre entirely too mature. I had to tell him that sensual content and sexual relationships in juvenile fiction lead to overly sexualized youth who are more easily susceptible to sexual exploitation.

I've listened to albums and approved some songs and not others based solely on lyrics. Even some Disney XD has been censored in our home all to protect my girls from being inundated with romance and relationships at too young of an age. Why else do eleven-year-olds think they should be dating? Ella once noticed that an entire class relationship (of two weeks) played out exactly like one of the Disney shows she had watched.

Mostly, we are helping her learn the balance of being fully who she is, in all her strength and athleticism and ambition without shaming and distancing boys. At a swim meet, we sat in the stands watching and waiting. Her event had been called, but she was the fourth heat. Near the dive blocks was a chin-up bar and she and some boys her age were kind of goofing around under the guise of warm-up. A boy agonizingly pulled himself up to the bar. One. The next boy got on. Three. And then she went. One. Two. Three. Four. Five...Twelve. She jumped down beaming.

From the rafters, we were simultaneously proud and smirking. In minutes, we knew, she would rub it in. The boys would try again, at least once, to prove themselves because surely they did it wrong the first time. Then she would show them again how much stronger she was, their arms still skinny and lanky without postpubescent muscle. One would mutter admiration. The others would scoff, shamed.

Inwardly, I smile that she can outrun, out push-up, and out pull-up the boys. But how do I fan the flame in such a way that those around her don't burn? It's not her responsibility to care for boys' egos, but what about being sensitive and spurring others on rather than gloating? She shouldn't have to squelch her speed, her knowledge, or her passion because it overwhelms the boys, but how can I teach her to be a confident and strong girl without a chip on her shoulder?

These were the thoughts and the conversations we had

around these issues leading up to *Becoming*. Having the conversation is the greatest win. Acknowledging we do not have all the answers as parents is disarming and reminds our kids, we are all learning here, doing what we hope is best, seeking God along the way. In the process of *Becoming*, we're on the journey together. Let's give each other grace and talk about it.

Questions for you:

1. What conversations have you and your daughter had around bodies, bras, besties, and boys?

2. How does your daughter feel about these four categories? Is there one that you need to address with more care than another?

3. What about your own story comes into play as you help your daughter engage hers?

4. How can you and your daughter journey through the process of becoming together?

Appendix B

From Her Dad to Dads

When you look at your sleeping daughter, you are confronted with a spiritual reality that you can't deny. A man can banter with his friends and colleagues about whether God exists. But a father looks at his daughter and knows.

—Meg Meeker[80]

If you are a father like me, you've been watching and waiting. From the moment your little girl entered the world, you felt the weight and responsibility to care for this treasure God entrusted to you. For dads like us, this is both wonderful and terrifying.

Now your little girl is becoming a woman. The inevitable transition into womanhood has arrived, and you stand at the precipice of yet another adventure in fathering. Too many dads completely miss it, and answer the phone in shock one day far too soon to the news of "We're getting married!"

---

80. Meg Meeker, *Strong Fathers, Strong Daughters: 10 Secrets Every Father Should Know* (New York: Ballantine, 2006), 199.

Other dads, out of fear rather than hope, hold her back and seek to contain her as long as possible, clipping her wings to prevent her from flying into womanhood.

But, if you are a father like me, you want something different for your girl. You know the magnificence of her strength and beauty. You want to be the kind of father who prepares her to soar, for you know the world needs her in all her glory, and it is your stewardship responsibility as her dad to aid in the unfurling of all God meant her to become.

As she walks through this *Becoming* year, our role as fathers is to establish for her the space to reveal her glory, to live into her beauty, and to discover her strength and voice. While the process is primarily led by her mother, your daughter needs to know your approval. She needs to see you creating the environment in which she can realize her glory. When she looks back from the edge of womanhood as her mother invites her to step forward into the company of women, she needs to see your kind, hopeful, and affirming eyes. As she takes flight, she does not need your leadership. She needs your blessing.

Dads, this can be difficult. I know a lot of men who are "take charge" kinds of guys, and out of (what I hope are) good intentions to lead the transition into womanhood, they end up steamrolling their daughters and wives. Rather than unveiling strength and glory, their daughters end up in fear of disappointing dad or insecure about her expression of her own heart.

We are called to be the kind of fathers who encourage our wives and daughters to fully explore womanhood. And let us join Ziauddin Yousafzai, Malala's father, in saying: "People ask me what is special about my mentorship that has made Malala so bold and courageous, vocal and poised. I tell them, 'Don't ask me what I did. Ask me what I did not do. I did not clip her wings, and that's all.' "[81]

Taking Flight—What Fathers Must Do

In my role as father, counselor, and leader of father-daughter experiences,[82] I have identified six key fathering actions essential to helping girls take flight into womanhood. Through these, fathers help create the honoring and approving environment necessary for *Becoming*.

Take Flight #1: Invitation

We all know the light in our children's eyes when fathers invite their children to be with them. Whether it's to donuts on Saturday morning or to climb a mountain, a girl's heart opens when her father invites her to be with him. Fathers, intentionally invite your daughters to be with you. Find those activities, places, or experiences she enjoys, and take her there. But remember, it's not about activities. It's about inviting her heart to come alive. She needs to know she is wanted.

Take Flight #2: Delight

Our eyes communicate more than we care to admit. Some of the deepest questions our daughters ask are, "Do you [Dad] delight in me? Do you see me as lovely

---

81. *TEDBlog*, "Why Is My Daughter Strong?" by Hailey Reissman, March 17, 2014, http://blog.ted.com/why-is-my-daughter-strong-because-i-didnt-clip-her-wings-ziauddin-yousafzai-at-ted2014/.

82. Restoration Project Experiences, www.restorationproject.net.

and delightful? When you consider me, do you experience joy?" Dads, far more than your provision of food, clothing, and a home, far more than good Christmas gifts or a new phone, your daughter wants your delight. Be intentional about showering her with your delighted eyes. This will ground her more than you can imagine.

Take Flight #3: Warmth

The world will attempt to chill her, shut her down and tell her she's either too much or not enough. We all know the world is not a warm place, especially for those girls who seek to find their strong voices and reveal the glory of God. More than your advice, direction, or leadership, she needs to know that you will always be there to melt away her fear, revitalize her frostbitten heart, and bring holy healing to the chill in her soul. She needs your warmth.

Take Flight #4: Humility

As your daughter makes the transition from girl to woman, an important shift must occur in your relationship. For the first many years of her life, she is your daughter. Her identity is shaped by her daughter-relationship to you and her mother. But as she discovers her voice, her identity is her own. As Malala's father says, "She became a very famous, very popular young girl. Before that, she was my daughter, but now I'm her father."[83] Will you have the humility to

---

83. *TEDBlog*, "Why Is My Daughter Strong?" by Hailey Reissman, March 17, 2014, http://blog.ted.com/why-is-my-daughter-strong-because-i-didnt -clip-her-wings-ziauddin-yousafzai-at-ted2014/.

step aside and allow your girl to truly become the centerpiece with her own identity and strength? She needs you to step aside so she can shine. That is the gospel call of fathering.

Take Flight #5: Kindness

I believe kindness is found at the intersection of strength and tenderness. While the word *nice* is never found in the Scriptures, kindness is everywhere. At the core, kindness holds solidity, weight, and truth together with gentleness, peace, and empathy. To be a kind father is to offer your daughter compassionate care with fortitude and strength. Throughout her life, the greatest invitation you can offer her is your kind response—not one that gives in to every request, nor one that rebuffs or refuses her. Will you be strong, and will you be gentle?

Take Flight #6: Blessing

Words are powerful and either offer life or mete out death. To bless our children is to 1) know their hearts intimately; 2) to have a vision for who God has created them to be; and 3) to speak forth a covering of hope and anticipation of who they are to become. During this year of becoming, will you speak intentional words of blessing over your daughter? They will be food for her soul.

The father who takes these six Take Flight actions seriously, while supporting and encouraging her mother in the process of *Becoming*, will create for them both the space to reveal their glory, to live into their beauty, and to discover their strong voices.

The Father's Story

Throughout *Becoming*, Beth has called mothers to address their own stories as they seek to raise their daughters. All intentional parenting must involve a deep exploration of our own life and story if there is ever a hope of helping locate our children in theirs. Men, this means one of the greatest fathering requirements on you is to find healing for yourself in the places where you are wounded so that you can be the kind of man you want to be for your kids.

You've likely heard the phrase, *Hurt people hurt people*. So much of our hurtful actions toward others stem from places of pain in our own hearts. We act (often subconsciously) out of the brokenness in our lives, and end up leaving emotional and relational debris in our wake.

There is another saying: *Transformed people transform people*. When we men have the courage to step into the fray and do the redemptive work of healing in our own lives and hearts, we have the capacity to offer massive transformation to the world around us. I have the privilege of working with many such brave men. And while the healing journey is hard, and the road to resurrection is always entered first through the doorway of death, the resulting restoration is glorious beyond comparison. I recently asked a man, "After all you've gone through to find healing—the dark nights, facing your pain, and struggling with your past—would you do it again?" His response: "Without question. Without doubt."

Fathers, you must attend to your own man hearts. Do so, and you will find the power to be transformational. Avoid it, and you will pass on your hurt for generations to come. Be a family-tree changer. Do the work.

Mothers Without Husbands and Daughters Without Fathers

Here's a reality. Far too many children live in fatherless homes, and far too many mothers carry the burden of parenting alone. My heart breaks for those of you who live this reality. Fathers are vital, and yet fatherlessness is a worldwide epidemic we must address. At the same time, we live in a world where women have brilliantly and valiantly navigated where men have abdicated or gone missing.

To you brave mothers who find yourselves alone on this journey, having been left, abandoned, or abused, I first want to apologize on behalf of all men. I am so deeply sorry. It is to you and for you that I dedicate my ministry's work of restoring men to be the men God designed and you deserve.

I ask that you not give up on men altogether. While you may be tempted to turn toward contempt, I beg of you instead to hold out hope. The hurt you have experienced is potentially beyond measure, and yet your daughter is watching you. With whatever reserves you may muster, I plead with you to seek out good men in your family, your church, your community, your schools. When no man is present for you, may you find men of courage to surround you and your daughter with kindness and safety. Seek out surrogate fathers, brothers, and uncles to be the dad your daughter needs.

To you brave mothers whose husbands have passed away, been deployed, or are otherwise unavailable to you in the high calling of parenting, I commend you. There are few more amazing people on this planet than those women who valiantly face the process of raising children amid loss. May you know the presence of the Father as you mother and father your kids.

You have already proved resilient and resourceful, and I

commend you for your bravery. Thank you for continuing to fight. Your deeds and your heart do not go unseen.

To the men who live in communities where women have been abused, abandoned, or left alone (whether literally or emotionally), I call on you to step up and step in. God has called all men to father, whether or not we have biological children. Fathering is in the heart of every man. Be fathers to your neighbors, your friends, your church community, your coworkers. Seek out ways to bring your fathering to bear on behalf of those who have no father. You are the answer to fatherlessness.

Let us raise a generation of girls who know the glory of God that is written into their lives and hearts, and may we all celebrate the moment a little girl finds her woman's voice.

Appendix C

Ideas to Fund a Rites of Passage

To be honest, pulling off a meaningful *Becoming* year does require strategy and sacrifice. Intentional parenting begins with intentional budgeting. Whether your expenses stop at books, movies, and a gift or include trips and activities, creating memories and crafting a thoughtful year will demand your time, resources, and creativity. I suspect some of you have already allowed dread to fill your hearts because your finances are simply not even close to create a year like this. Fellow sojourner, I know what it is to live lean. I too have lived through seasons of chest-tightening, teeth-gritting panic over the cost of school pictures, field trips, and the endless next size of shoes. I have ideas for you.

My husband and I put ourselves through graduate school debt free (with three children) by employing some crazy moneymaking strategies. It did require enormous creativity and a sacrifice of time on our part, but the reward was well worth the investment. Now, having created rites of passage years for two of our children, we have even more ideas for how any parent can earn some extra money to make this year special. Think of your skills, stuff, and savings.

Skills

1. Swapping skills. Let's say your brakes need repairing. There goes the six hundred dollars you had saved for *Becoming*! Isn't this how it always happens? But as you talk with your car mechanic, you learn that his daughter is getting married. You have a background in flower arrangement, or event planning, or catering, or photography and he's willing to trade services. You get the idea. What skills do you have that you can trade for services that would otherwise have cost you money?

2. Skill-based jobs. Speaking of skills, what can you do in your current life to earn extra money? My husband earned money for our son's year by doing outdoor lawn care for his father's rental properties. I paid for a semester of grad school by cleaning a friend's mother's home once a week. Humbling? Yes, get over it. Are you home with a younger child? Could you also nanny? Do you have pets? Could you sign up on dogvacay.com to provide pet sitting? Can you tutor Spanish? Teach piano?

3. Short-term jobs. Perhaps you have the time to truly take on a small, part-time job. Uber and Lyft offer flexible earnings that can fit into anyone's schedule. Substitute teaching. Pizza delivery. With a master's and at the age of thirty-five, my husband found himself hanging up long underwear at a retail store to earn extra cash. I cleaned a hair salon in exchange for free haircuts!

Stuff

1. Sell. Most of us have too much of everything. While some of our things are only worthy of the trash, some items could sell at a garage sale. Other possessions could sell on eBay or Craigslist. What is collecting dust on your shelves or hasn't seen the light of day in years? How many unused bikes still hang from your garage rafters? Become a master of selling your stuff.

2. Share. In today's sharing economy, almost any possession can be "shared" for a price. I funded this *Becoming* year through HomeAway. We listed our home to rent and were amazed at how many people needed a place to stay for graduation, weddings, and sports tournaments. You can do the same thing with your car in some cities and at many airports.

3. Swap. Are you a DIYer? Can you take a beat-up table and repurpose it? Every summer our neighborhood brings in a large dumpster and we watch people throw in tables, chairs, and furniture. More than a few times, we've raided the dump, painted and repaired the items, and sold them on Craigslist a few days later.

Savings

1. Shrink payments. Consider your budget and ways you can cut monthly spending in order to save. Cable, Netflix, Hulu Plus, a landline, et cetera, are all luxuries that could easily save a hundred dollars a month. Perhaps you can refinance your home or find cheaper automobile insurance. Maybe the whole family takes a season off of sports? Are you driving around a car that could be downgraded? Oftentimes, huge savings are available when we alter our lifestyle a little. Our family has done all of the above (except, we've never owned a car worth downgrading!).

2. Savings delay. This may be incredibly unpopular and maybe unwise, but if you're saving for retirement or even college, perhaps pause for a bit. I tend to believe that a rites of passage year has a lasting investment in your daughter's life that is worth the sacrifice of other savings in the meantime.

3. Super savings. The biggest expense for my daughter's *Becoming* year was the travel. Of course, not every mom needs to replicate a big trip. I am often so excited about the memory making that I move forward with plans and then have to find a way to make it happen. Mileage credit cards have been fabulous! Again, not everyone will agree, but I love getting thirty thousand miles just for signing up and then using it for everything to add up the points. We have flown free this way. Other cards offer hotel points in the same way. Sometimes family members are happy to gift their hotel points (have you asked?). Consider staying with friends or even friends of friends for a special trip. For our trip to the Netherlands, I joined a bike club that allowed us to stay with Dutch people for only nineteen euros per night, including breakfast.

I want to challenge you to figure out how to make this happen. Please do not assume that your finances prohibit you from crafting an amazing *Becoming* year for your daughter. Pray about what you want and need to do for her. Make a budget and then ask God to supply what you need. Accept that it is going to take planning, strategizing, and sacrifice on your part. You may be stretched personally to think outside of the box and risk your pride. And to that, I remind you, we are all in the process of becoming. This year is as much about you as it is about her. Embrace the beautiful struggle of bringing forth a woman. I guarantee you it is so, so worth it!

Appendix D

Resources and Alternate Ideas

I'll be the first to admit my interest in Afghanistan and Holocaust history is unusual. The books, films, and experiences I did with my daughter are reflections of my own interests, but I also tried to adapt to hers. When she could not get into *Little Women* or Chelsea Clinton's, *It's Your World*, I flexed. We watched *Hiding Place* and *Anne Frank* instead of reading the books. The subtitled French film *Of Gods and Men* was not a hit. But pushing her to read things she typically would never read has altered her life. Rifqa Bary's and Katie Davis's memoirs reached parts of her soul our conversations would not have reached. *Skateistan* gave her a visual of what creative consistency can do for underprivileged children.

I encourage you to start with your own interests, because passion will augment every experience. From there, get creative. Who are your heroines? Who would you like to learn more about? What is coming to theaters (e.g., we read *I Am Malala*, then went to hear her speak, then ditched school to see the documentary, *He Named Me Malala*)? And don't forget to crowd source: Ask your people what they're reading, watching, and learning about.

The list I provide below is a crowd-sourced list of ideas similar to the ones I chose. Recognizing how vastly different we are as moms, I hope this serves to give you plenty of ideas or jog your thinking toward others.

Films

Queen of Katwe—a Kenyan girl from the slums becomes a national chess champion

Hidden Figures—the story of African-American "computers" in the rise of NASA

The Eagle Huntress—a thirteen-year-old Mongolian girl becomes the first eagle hunter

Lord of the Rings trilogy

A Little Princess

Rogue One: A Star Wars Story

Narnia series

Documentaries on current events

Books for Girls

Little Women, Hiding Place, Diary of Anne Frank (all books with movie versions)

Girls Who Rocked the World by Michelle Roehm McCann and Amelie Welden

Rise of the Rocket Girls: The Women Who Propelled Us, from Missiles to the Moon to Mars by Nathalia Holt

Hidden Girl: The True Story of a Modern-Day Child Slave by Shyima Hall

The Dressmaker of Khair Khana by Gayle Tzemach Lemmon

10 Ultimate Truths Girls Should Know by Kari Kampakis

10 Things for Teen Girls by Kate Conner

Graceful: Letting Go of Your Try-Hard Life by Emily P. Freeman

Women in Science: 50 Fearless Pioneers Who Changed the World by Rachel Ignotofsky

Do Hard Things: A Teenage Rebellion Against Low Expectations by Alex Harris

Miracle on Voodoo Mountain: A Young Woman's Remarkable Story of Pushing Back the Darkness for the Children of Haiti by Megan Boudreaux

Experiences that Become Metaphors

- Olympic trials or a championship game of her favorite sport: how can she use her skill to benefit others?
- Backstage passes to her favorite band/artist: how was *she* designed to offer beauty?
- Day at the Capitol with a congressperson: how will she use *her* voice to make a difference?
- Enter a race together (bike, run, swim, Tough Mudder): reaching the finish line takes perseverance
- Wear the same dress for a month while raising awareness and/or funds: sometimes we sacrifice for the sake of others
- Sleep outside with a homeless solidarity event: learning the difference between empathy and sympathy
- Craft an *Amazing Race*– or *Survivor*–type test: how is life like the *Amazing Race*?
- Scavenger hunt in a mega city or in an art museum: discovering the mystery requires clues
- Comic Con: she too has a gift that is unique
- Lego Land: build a strong foundation

Websites

Amightygirl.com
Itsyourworld.com

Projectinspired.com
Nwhm.org (National Women's History Museum)
Makers.com (a collection of videos about women)

Books about Parenting Girls

Queen Bees and Wannabes: Helping Your Daughter Survive Cliques, Gossip, Boys, and the New Realities of Girl World by Rosalind Wiseman

So Sexy So Soon: The New Sexualized Childhood and What Parents Can Do to Protect Their Kids by Diane E. Levin and Jean Kilbourne

Untangled: Guiding Teenage Girls Through the Seven Transitions into Adulthood by Lisa Damour

How Children Raise Parents: The Art of Listening to Your Family by Dan Allender

Help for Parents

Parenting coaching—www.restorationcounselingnoco.com/parent-coaching

Pop culture translation for parents—www.axis.org/ct

Online and social media safety—www.connectsafely.org

Appendix E

Blank Charts for Planning

Becoming Category	Working Definition	Time Frame	Who Else?

Category:

Books for Her to Read	Books I'm Reading	Scripture	Films to Watch	Activities	Gift

About the Author

Credit: Jenni Lillie

BETH BRUNO is the mother of three children, including two daughters. She has been in ministry for twenty years, including ten years internationally with Cru. She founded A Face to Reframe, a nonprofit organization to prevent human trafficking, and regularly speaks and trains around the topic of trafficked youth. She speaks at women's retreats around the topic of "Women Becoming" and finds support from being a member of Redbud Writers Guild, an international organization for expanding the Christian feminine voice. Beth writes regularly for well-read publications, including *Relevant*, *Today's Christian Woman*, *The Well*, *Mudroom* blog, and *Thrive*. You can find her at bethbruno.org.

A VOICE BECOMING Field Notes

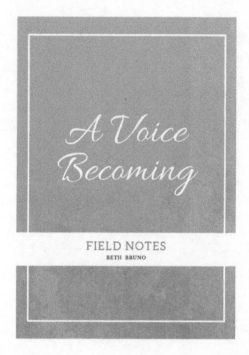

Are you ready to begin designing a Becoming year for your daughter? The 30-page companion Field Notes guides readers through their own story, goes deeper into the questions asked at the end of each chapter in the book, and provides detailed categories to create a unique Becoming year.

Download yours for free: www.avoicebecoming.com.